For Makiya

In all of us there is a hunger, marrow deep, to know our heritage—to know who we are and where we came from. Without this enriching knowledge, there is a hollow yearning. No matter what our attainments in life, there is still a vacuum, an emptiness, and the most disquieting loneliness.

—ALEX HALEY

Table of Contents

Acknowledgements

I am forever thankful to have grown up with parents who loved me unconditionally and took pride in every one of my accomplishments. They've been gone for almost thirty years and I miss them still. I hope they would they would be proud of this accomplishment too.

I must acknowledge the Saskatchewan Post-Adoption Department and those individuals who were instrumental in giving me back my identity: Walter Andres, Bernice Donnelly, and Bev Jaigobin. Although the phone calls and letters we shared may have been just part of your everyday job, to me they were life-changers. Thank you from the bottom of my heart.

Many thanks to Susan Albert, the board, and members, of the Story Circle Network for all of the resources they provide to help women tell the stories of their lives. Without this organization I might never have found the confidence to write this book.

Thanks to my local Story Circle sisters, especially my critique partners Heather Stinson and Liz Kranz. You heard many of the early chapters of this book and helped me see where I needed to tighten, clarify, and let go of pieces of the story. I treasure our Saturday morning coffee times.

Kathleen Kelly, thank you for helping me find the structure of this book, your encouragement, and editorial expertise were invaluable.

Jennifer Lauck, Judy Miller, Kim Richardson, and Nancy Verrier: thank you taking time to read and comment on my manuscript.

I am thankful for the work done by my cousins Esther Zaccharias and Cindy Mosher. Thanks to them I have a family tree dating back to the 1600s. Not bad for someone who once had no idea where she came from! Wendy, Ruth, and Miriam: I treasure our sisterhood. Lori: thank you for being part of my life; though our lives have taken different paths I will always remember times gone by. Frank, Ed, Merlin, Don: I wish we could have had more time.

Special love and thanks to my immediate family. Laurinda and Michael, you were, and always will be, the best of me. Brandon and Todd, the sons I gained when I married your Dad: there was a special place in my heart just waiting for both of you. Nicole, Gord, and Robyn, my son-and-daughters-in-love: each of you blesses me in your own unique way and I'm honored to have each of you in my life. My grandchildren, Jaxon, Makiya, and the little one who will have found a way into Grandma's arms by the time this book is published: you are the ultimate joys of my life; I hope this story becomes part of your story.

Finally, my deep gratitude to my husband who believed I had a story worth telling and was endlessly patient with me as I sequestered myself in my "woman cave" to write.

Thank you, honey for your patience, encouragement, and wisdom. Thank you for listening to and reading my story. And thank you for your understanding about every 'PID' email I sent you over the past few years. I love you seven.

A Note from the Author

Sometimes I worry that talking about how being adopted has impacted me might send the wrong message. It's true that the person I grew up to be was shaped, in no small way, by the fact that I was removed from my family of origin and adopted by another family. I struggled as a child, as a teenager, as a young adult, and as an adult, wondering who I was supposed to be and where I fit in. I have had a sense of shame at my core, not for anything I did but for who I am. I have been terrified of being abandoned, and this fear has contributed to some poor choices. I have felt rejected, legitimately or not, by many or most of the people who have passed through my life. I have been plagued with deep and unresolved grief, a grief I didn't even realize was there. I tread softly and leave a small footprint because of a sense of not being entitled to what other people are entitled to. I have felt alienated and alone. I have wondered who I would be if not for being an adoptee.

But I also have been abundantly blessed.

I had parents who loved me and gave me a good life. They supported me, they believed in me, and they loved me. I had an extended family who embraced me, and I knew what it felt like to be surrounded by people who loved me. I rarely have wanted for anything I needed, I have had good health, I have a husband who loves me, and I have happy and healthy children and grandchildren.

But just like you, I deserve to know where my ancestors came from. I deserve to be mirrored by others who resemble me physically, in mannerisms, in interests, and in talents. I am entitled to know if there is a history of illness in my lineage or of greatness passed down from generation to generation. I deserve to know the name I was given when I was born.

The wound left in my soul from not having these things will never completely heal, but in learning the truth, I have found comfort and peace and learned to release much of the grief that has gnawed at me silently, just below the surface, for much of my life. I know these things are true because I have been fortunate enough to gain access to my family of origin. I now know the name I was given at birth and have looked into the faces of people who share my DNA. More importantly, I have learned the truth about the circumstances surrounding my birth and subsequent adoption; I have found a measure of peace and healing.

Please understand that I believe in the blessing of adoption. Through adoption, children are given a mom and dad, parents are blessed by the precious children entrusted to their care, and families are created. I am thankful that, for the most part, adoption is no longer mired in a culture of secrecy and shame. I am thrilled with the openness I see the adoption community slowly embracing and happy for the adoptees of today, who will not only know the love of adoptive parents but will also—when the time is right—have access to information about their families of origin and may even grow up knowing some of their biological family members. All this honesty can only contribute to making the lives of everyone in the adoption constellation healthier; secrets are never the best option.

I am grieved that some still believe it's okay to keep such secrets and deny adoptees like me access to information about who we are and where we came from. We cannot reach our full human potential if we are kept in the dark. As someone who was adopted under the closed adoption system, I understand the damage that secrecy and lies can have on the psyche, and I believe it's up to those of us who have been fortunate enough to obtain the basic information still denied to so many adoptees to speak out about the healing that truth can bring.

I also believe that it's our responsibility to be respectful and thoughtful in this work, and for that reason, I have changed the names of some of the characters in this book. This story is mine, to the best of my memory, and there is no need for me to call attention to specific people who may remember things differently than I do. In some cases, I have taken literary license in creating composite characters.

I'm convinced that change in the adoption mosaic will come with education and that those who have been impacted by the closed system have the most responsibility to educate those who do not understand.

Linda Hoye 2011

Prologue

January 2, 2009

*G*radually I become conscious of a male voice speaking quietly next to me. It's 4:45 a.m., and the NPR commentator is telling me it's time for the day to begin. I slowly surface from the comfort of sleep. She's an elusive visitor these days and I'm reluctant to leave her behind. Between relentless hot flashes, emotional stress, and what my doctor is now calling neuropathic pain, I sleep fitfully when I sleep at all.

I reach over, turn off the clock radio, toss back the covers, and fling my legs out of the warmth of my bed, leaving my husband and our sleeping Yorkies, Chelsea and Maya, behind. The moment my feet hit the floor, my mind is at work thinking about the day's priorities. I have an almost obsessive personal need to exceed expectations. In times of quiet reflection, I admit to myself that the high standards I set for myself are driven by insecurity and a need to prove my personal worth. Most of the time, however, I'm too focused on the task at hand to give it much thought.

On this morning, the second day of a new year, I stand before the mirror and lean forward for a better look. I'm nearsighted, and without the help of my contact lenses or glasses, the world is a blurry place. I'm a few weeks away from my fiftieth birthday, and with every passing day, my face seems to show more evidence of that looming milestone.

I fill the sink with warm water and dip my washcloth a few times. Some women say that at a certain point in life they see their mother's face looking back at them in the mirror. If the woman who gave birth to me is there, I don't recognize her. As an adoptee, that's one of many disadvantages that frustrate me as I experience the inevitable changes that come with aging. I have no one to talk to about my menopausal symptoms. What is normal for the gene pool I come from? Have all the women in my family had to deal with the relentless and overwhelming "power surges" that keep me awake at night? How long did they last?

I lift the wet facecloth to my face and hold it there for a few moments, taking comfort in the warmth of the cloth and the sanctuary it provides. After taking a few deep breaths, I shake my head to clear the cobwebs. Grabbing two fluffy, blue bath towels, I head into the tiny closet-like room that houses the shower and the toilet. I like the security of that room; it's like a white womb protecting and shielding me from harm.

Later, with one towel wrapped around my body and the second wrapped like a turban on my head, I step out of the shower room and find, as I do every morning, that my husband, Gerry, has left me a creamy French-vanilla-flavored mug of coffee on the vanity. I take the first sip and let out an involuntary "mmm," thankful for his gesture. He is one of the many blessings I'm thankful for.

Just before 6:00 a.m., as I'm throwing a Lean Cuisine into my tote bag and getting ready to race out the door for work, the phone rings. It's my daughter, Laurinda.

"We're going to the hospital," she tells me quietly when I pick up the phone; I can hear weariness as her voice breaks. "I'm scared," she confesses.

I nod to my husband, confirming to him it's the phone call we've been waiting for as I sit down on a kitchen chair. I wish I could reach through the telephone line to wrap my arms around her; instead, I wrap my arms around myself in a vicarious attempt to embrace her from afar. I lean over while I talk to her and try to ease her fears. I remember that combination of fear and giddy excitement I felt thirty years earlier when I went to the hospital to bring her into the world. In some ways it seems like just yesterday; in others it is like a lifetime ago.

"I know, sweetie. You'll be okay. Try and relax, okay? I know you're tired, but you're almost there, and pretty soon you'll have that beautiful baby you've been waiting for!"

We've both been waiting. I'm overjoyed at the prospect of becoming a grandmother.

"I love you, Laurinda. I'll be there as soon as I can, okay?"

When I'm satisfied I've reassured her as much as I can, we end our call. I hug my husband, and together we pray for Laurinda, her husband, Gord, and the baby on the way. Then I do a little dance I've perfected over the past nine months and dubbed the "grandma dance." After I finish my silly jig, I race upstairs to my office where I log on to my computer and search for the earliest flight that will take me from Seattle, Washington, to Calgary, Alberta. I don't think twice as I enter my credit card numbers on the airline website to pay the exorbitant fee for a last-minute reservation; nothing could stop me from being there to welcome my grandchild into the world.

Six hours later I've gone from a dark and rainy Pacific Northwest morning to a frigid-but-sunny Canadian afternoon. As I hurry across the snowy parking lot of the Calgary Foothills Hospital, the crunching sound of my boots on the snow reminds me that even though I feel like I'm walking on air, I'm firmly planted smack-dab in the middle of one of the coldest days of the year.

The hospital lobby is alive with activity and filled with the smiling faces of people carrying stuffed animals, balloons, and flowers. My gaze rests on other women who appear to be near my age, and I share a subtle smile with them. I feel like I'm about to become a new member of an exclusive club I've longed to join, and the "grandma smile" is like the secret handshake.

When I arrive on the labor and delivery floor and locate the swinging doors that lead me toward pending grandma-hood, I shove them open and confidently step into the ward. The nurse at the desk looks up and inquires if I am the mother of an expectant mother on the ward.

Can't you tell by the crazy grin on my face? I want to ask her, but instead I just smile my goofy grandma smile and nod.

Laurinda is in her room, wearing a blue cotton hospital gown and propped up in a hospital bed. Her long blonde hair is pulled back, her eyes are weary, and her face is puffy, but she returns my smile and lifts her arms for my embrace. Gord's unshaven face breaks into a wide grin when he sees me. He has a video camera and is narrating as he records the events of the day; he puts it down long enough to give me a welcoming hug.

Motherhood isn't coming easily to my daughter. The journey just to get to this day has been long and arduous, and she tells me she is experiencing the dreaded back labor and has just been given her second epidural. Her struggle continues.

Beneath the blue blanket that covers her ample belly, I can see the outline of a baby monitor encircling her girth. Next to the bed, a monitor spits out a white paper tongue that shows the strength of her contractions. I pull it out to get a better look at the lines it draws; there are peaks and valleys, like a roadmap the baby is following on its journey to get here.

"It looks like that last one was a good one," I say to Laurinda.

She grins. "What is your definition of good?"

In an alcove next to the bed, I see a metal, table-like contraption with an overhead heater. A nurse with laughing eyes and a brown ponytail, whom Gord introduces as Billie, is spreading flannel sheets on top of the silver cradle that will soon hold a baby. The sight of the baby heater somehow makes everything seem more real. My daughter is about to become a mother. I am about to become a grandmother.

———

After a few hours pass, Laurinda's contractions intensify. She lies on her side facing Gord, her head tucked into the corner of the bed, and she breathes through an oxygen mask she holds to her face. The wheezing sound mingles with her own low, deep moan to create a birthday song that croons the time is drawing near for a new life to be born. Gord gently strokes her back and whispers words of encouragement.

I am struck yet again with how my daughter leans on her husband for support. It's something I struggle with. My own independent spirit and need to be in control make it difficult for me to lean on anyone for anything.

Perhaps my daughter is stronger than I am, as she has learned how to be both strong and vulnerable; it's something I've come to admire in her.

After checking on Laurinda's progress, Nurse Billie smooths the blue blanket back over her legs and declares it's time for her to start pushing. My daughter, a private person like me, told me weeks ago that she only wanted Gord to be present for the actual delivery. I understand her request perfectly, and I kiss her forehead, hug Gord, and retreat to the tiny waiting room, where my mind goes back to the day I was the woman giving birth to her first child.

"Push! Come on, you can do it! Keep pushing! Look down here at the mirror; the baby is coming!" The delivery room nurse urges me to look toward the mirror positioned at the end of the bed.

"I can't see! I don't have my glasses on." Why didn't someone tell me that I'd need my glasses? I give one more push with everything that's left in me and feel my baby slip from my body.

The doctor says, "It's a girl!"

They lay her on my chest, and I look into the eyes of a beautiful, dark-haired, reddish-skinned, screaming infant. My daughter! Laurinda! As I look into Laurinda's eyes and the nurse calls me "Mom," everything falls away. All that matters is the beautiful baby in my arms.

Two years later, my son Michael was born. My body remembers the sensation of contractions and the work of pushing him out into the world, too. My heart remembers the miracle of those moments when I saw each of them for the first time: Laurinda, red-faced and crying, and Michael, paler and quiet. I recall minute details about each of their faces, my beautiful babies. They were the first human beings I ever laid eyes on who were my flesh and blood.

Occasionally I still wonder if anyone remembers the moment I came into the world, though I rarely think about my own birth. My life began when I was adopted. There was no one to tell me stories about the day I was born. My emergence into this life was shrouded in mystery and shame. I have a sensation sometimes that I wasn't born, just dropped here from outer space.

There are windows in the swinging doors between the waiting room and the labor and delivery ward. Though my mind wanders, I keep an eye on those windows. Each sound from behind the doors makes me stand and look down the hall in the direction of Laurinda's room. Time seems strangely altered. Have hours passed or only minutes? Finally I see Gord striding down the hall, a smile the size of the Bow River on his face.

"It's a girl!" he exclaims as he pushes through the doors. "And she's beautiful!"

"Congratulations, Dad!" I throw my arms around him and offer a silent prayer of thanks while I follow him back down the hall, wiping tears from my eyes

Laurinda is sitting up in bed, smiling and crying at the same time. She looks more tired than she did earlier, but there is an indescribable glow about her

"Congratulations, Mommy!" I embrace her and kiss her forehead.

Satisfied that she is okay, I turn toward the baby warmer. Nurse Billie is bustling about, and Gord is videotaping again. They clear a path for me to get closer to the warmer. My granddaughter, eyes wide open, is looking around as if to take in the sights of this new world she has arrived in.

I reach over and gently take her tiny hand in mine as I lean over and whisper so only she can hear. "Welcome! We've been waiting for you."

Prologue

I'm sitting in a chair holding my newborn granddaughter, who has been given the name Makiya Rose, while the nurses fuss around, tending to her mom. My heart is so full it aches as I hold the perfect baby girl in my arms, stroke her soft little hands, drink in the features of her exquisite little face, and gently stroke her reddish hair. My eyes move back and forth between the flawless baby girl in my arms and my daughter in the hospital bed in front of me.

Makiya will never have reason to think she was dropped here on Earth from outer space; we will tell and retell the story of this day. We will share with her the ultrasound pictures taken when the features of a baby were first identifiable, and together we'll watch the video taken while she was still in utero that shows her moving and even sucking on her thumb. In the years to come, we will tell her about the months when she grew in her mommy's belly and how her mommy's countenance softened as she prepared to welcome her. We will tell her how her mommy, daddy, and whole extended family anticipated her arrival.

And just for an instant, a flash of grief passes through my mind for baby Linda and the stories that were never told about my birth. Joy must have been noticeably absent on the January day when I was born. As quickly as it came, the thought is gone, and I return to the present and the baby girl in my arms.

———◆———

At first Makiya's age is measured in minutes, then hours, and finally days. When she is three weeks old, my own age changes decades as I turn fifty. I let Gerry know weeks in advance that I don't want any fuss over my birthday. He gives me a beautiful card with some hundred-dollar bills tucked inside that are meant to be used for a flight back to Calgary. I haven't stopped talking about the beautiful Makiya since I got home; he knows I'm eager to return.

"Isn't she beautiful?" I ask repeatedly when we flip through the photographs I took in the days following her birth.

He always responds affirmatively, though sometimes not quite vehemently enough for my liking.

"No, really," I press him. "Isn't she really the most beautiful baby girl you have ever seen?"

"She's beautiful," he concurs, and I'm satisfied until the next time I go through the pictures.

For a number of years, a sense of melancholy has fallen over me on my birthday. I insist on minimal celebration: phone calls from my children and a card and flowers from my husband are enough. "It's just another day," I insist.

Yet every year, at some point on the anniversary of the day I was born, I am overtaken with sadness that I have only recently been able to explain. This year especially, when I consider the joy in the delivery room a few weeks earlier when Makiya was born, I am grieved. I'd grown up hearing I was "chosen" by my parents. But I was only available to be chosen because I was first cast away by the woman who was supposed to love me the most, the woman whose heartbeat I had grown used to during the months when I grew in her womb, the woman whose ancestors were mine, whose features shaped mine, whose characteristics and mannerisms were interjected into my being at the moment I was conceived, the woman who thought there was something so wrong with me that she rejected me permanently from the beginning.

Every year on my birthday, the underlying sense of sorrow and my desire for the day to pass unnoticed is coupled with a sense of wanting to be special, of wishing I was special, and at the same time wishing I wasn't.

The Nature of an Adopted Child

The quiet, compliant adoptee believes she always has to please others, to be very, very careful not to offend others or put herself in a position to be criticized or shunned. She becomes the people pleaser, never having a diverse opinion, always trying to fit into every situation in which she finds herself. Yet she feels as if she fits into none of them. She may believe herself to be introverted and shy. She may try not to be too visible.

—NANCY VERRIER, *COMING HOME TO SELF*

Ed and Laura

For most women, the telltale signs of impending motherhood are the changes in their bodies: their breasts become fuller and more tender, their bellies swell, and they have morning sickness and afternoon fatigue. My mom, Laura Brauer, likely got the news in a phone call to the house my dad built in Moose Jaw, Saskatchewan. I imagine her at twenty-nine, putting down the black telephone receiver and only then allowing excitement to take hold. Years of waiting and frustration at the doctors' failure to determine the cause of her childlessness were about to be over.

Mom grew up during the Great Depression on the hot, windy, dusty Saskatchewan prairie. Her father died of pneumonia when she was barely two years old, leaving my grandma to raise Mom, her older brother, Albert, and their infant sister, Edith (whom they called Edie), on her own. Grandpa's family, the Sellsteds, took care of their own, and his parents built a tiny house adjacent to their own in the tiny hamlet of Benson, Saskatchewan, for Grandma and her children. Grandma lived in that one-room house until she died at seventy-five, and apart from the time he was away in the war, Uncle Albert also lived there until he died. When I was a child, we spent many summer days in Benson visiting my unlovable, cranky grandma, my jovial uncle, and his scrappy black dog, Sport.

Dad grew up in Moose Jaw, the only son in a family of seven children. Grandpa Brauer was a carpenter and a hard-drinking man who tried the patience of his good-natured, plump, and happy wife, Helena. I have only vague memories of Grandpa; he died when I was five. By all accounts Dad had a typical boyhood: he had a faithful dog named Mac who followed him everywhere, he delivered newspapers, he was a Boy Scout and a member of the YMCA, and he went swimming at the new Natatorium—the Nat— that was built when he was fourteen years old.

Mom was still a teenager and Dad an attractive thirty-year-old just back from fighting overseas in World War II when they met at a dance in a neighboring village. Dad was working as a bookkeeper at the fledgling Graham Construction Company, and he was drawn to the fresh-faced young prairie girl. He promised that he would give her three things if she would agree to be his wife: a house, a diamond ring, and a fur coat.

Mom and Dad were married at the majestic St. Andrew's church in Moose Jaw, and soon afterward, on weekends and after work, Dad began construction of their home on Seventh Avenue North West in Moose Jaw. In time, he saved enough money to fulfill his other promises and presented her with a three-quarter-carat diamond solitaire and a black, full-length, sealskin fur coat.

Over the course of the next ten years, Mom and Dad created a comfortable middle-class life and accumulated all the material things they needed. They were a fun-loving couple, hosting parties in their new house on the weekends, where they danced to "Goodnight Irene" and "The Tennessee Waltz" played on scratchy 78-rpm records. Dad sometimes drank too much, but everybody did now and then; it was no cause for concern.

When years passed and they remained childless, friends began to joke that they enjoyed the party life too much to ever have children. Even Dad's mother prophesied that they'd never be parents. She died before the phone call came that proved her wrong, the call that announced to Mom that a four-month-old baby girl was available for adoption.

I was chubby and wide-eyed and wearing a pretty blue dress when I was placed into the arms of my new mommy. Mom was a calm and capable first-time mother, having had plenty of experience caring for baby cousins when she was growing up in Benson, and Dad was as proud as could be of his new daughter. He snapped photograph after photograph of me sitting in my little car seat next to a smiling Laura in the front seat of their blue Buick.

After the prescribed period of probation in Mom and Dad's home, my birth certificate was amended to show my new name: Linda Gail Brauer.

The names of my birth parents were replaced with Mom's and Dad's names. My original birth certificate was sealed; in effect, it was if my birth parents had never existed.

I was adopted, not born.

Illusion of Truth

"*W*hat are you doing, Linda?"

"I'm getting in the backseat to make room for the baby,"
I say as I crawl over the car seat.

I have a vague recollection of my two-year-old self climbing into the
backseat while Mom settled the new baby in a blue car bed on the front
seat, but as I've gotten older, I've begun to doubt the memory and wonder
if it only seems like a memory because Mom and Dad told me the story so
often. Perhaps it was one of the stories that well-meaning social workers
told adoptive parents to tell their children to help them learn to accept a
second child into the family, much like the "chosen baby" story.

"We went to a place where there were many different babies, and when
we came to you, you lifted your arms toward us, and that's how we knew
that you were the baby for us. We chose you out of a whole bunch of other
babies."

I chose my parents, and they chose me; we were meant to be a family.

"If anyone teases you about being adopted, you just tell them that other
kids' parents had to take them, but we chose you.

Lesson intended: I am special. I was chosen.

There is never an official "adoption talk," but I always know in some
sense that I am adopted in the same way I instinctively know that it is not
okay to ask questions or probe too deeply on the subject.

Lesson learned: I am different. I wasn't always part of this family. There is a secret attached to my being born.

"Is that the truth, Linda?"

It is a hot summer afternoon, and Mom is taking a bath while baby Lori naps. I am playing quietly on the rug outside the bathroom door, which she has left slightly ajar. I am content to sit with my favorite Little Golden Books until I hear Lori stir in her crib.

I set my books aside and tiptoe into the darkened bedroom we share. Lori is sitting up in her crib. She breaks into a smile when she sees me. I put my foot on the bottom of the crib rail, pull myself up, and crawl into the crib with her. We play together for a few minutes; I like the coziness and security of the crib.

Then I get an idea of how to surprise Mom.

I step back over the rail of the crib and down onto the rug. I manage to lower the side rail and pull Lori out of the crib and down onto the rug with me, all the while cautioning her with my finger to my lips to "sh." I run to the bathroom, leaving her sitting on the rug, and push open the door.

"Mommy, the baby crawled out of her crib!"

By this time Lori has crawled into the bathroom—evidence that she has indeed managed to climb out of her crib by herself—and that's when Mom asks if I am telling the truth.

The excitement I felt about surprising her evaporates immediately and is replaced with a heavy lump in the pit of my stomach. As soon as I confess the truth, the uncomfortable feeling goes away.

Lesson learned: not telling the truth makes my tummy hurt.

I am seven years old and playing outside when Susan Gregor tells me Santa Claus isn't real. I am indignant and run home to find Mom to ask her to set Susan straight.

"Mom, Susan told me there is no such thing as Santa Claus. Can you please tell her that he is real?

Mom stops what she is doing and turns from the sink, drying her hands on a dish towel.

"Linda, I can't tell a lie. Santa Claus is just a fairy tale."

I am not upset by this revelation; in fact, I feel like I have been inducted into a club for big girls.

Lesson learned: my mom always tells the truth.

———◆———

Always tell the truth. Honesty is the best policy. That sinking feeling in the pit of your stomach will not be there if you are truthful.

These are the lessons I learn at an early age. I want to do the right thing and I always try to tell the truth; I don't like the uncomfortable sensation in my stomach that deception causes. Yet there are secrets all around me.

I develop persistent stomachaches. Mom takes me to the doctor repeatedly in an attempt to get to the source of the pain, but despite many exams and tests, the doctor never finds anything physically wrong with me.

———◆———

"Play 'Down Yonder,' princess,"

We are downstairs in the rumpus room: Dad, me, my friend Joan, and Joan's dad. I am eleven years old, and it's unusual for me to have a friend over to play indoors. This day is all the more unusual because Joan's dad is there. It's important to me that we have a good time. Although I have fun playing Barbies with Joan, I'm tense all the while, my guard never completely down. I'm not used to having my friends around my family. I'm afraid she will see something in our house, our family, and mostly in me that will make her stop being my friend. I just want everything to seem normal.

The men are enjoying a drink, likely rye and water, though it is the middle of the day. Dad's drinking is one of the unspoken secrets in our home, and today it's out in the open. I'm humiliated. The fact that Joan's dad is joining him diminishes my embarrassment just a little.

Dad is tenacious about things he's fond of, be it a drink or a favorite song. "Down Yonder," a polka, is one of his favorites; he plays the scratchy 78 over and over. One day I asked Mrs. Knight, my piano teacher, to teach me to play it as a surprise for him. Ever since my surprise was revealed, Dad frequently requests a command performance, and I've begun to despise the song and rue the day I learned it. Playing the song repeatedly for Dad's pleasure is one thing, but playing it in front of others is something else altogether.

I should have known Dad would ask me to play the stupid song for Joan's dad. He always acts so proud and pleased when I play it and showers me with praise when I'm finished. I know my rendition isn't that good, which makes Dad's praise seem insincere. I'd rather sit quietly playing Barbies with Joan and blend into the room as much as possible. But ever the obedient child, I climb to my feet, walk to the out-of-tune black upright Willis piano, and take my place on the bench. My fingers begin to move choppily over the piano keys.

For a time, my audience of three listens silently. Then, out of the blue, Joan blurts out, "Linda told me she was adopted."

I am mortified. My heart beats faster and the room seems suddenly warmer. What will happen now?

As I continue to play, I hear Joan's dad ask, "Do you know what adoption means, Joan?"

"Oh, yes," she responds. "It means that your real parents didn't want you, so they gave you away to another family, and they became your parents."

I finish the song and sit quietly on the black piano bench, wondering what to do next.

"Did you hear that, princess?" Dad asks sharply.

In that moment, I have to make a choice. I can respond affirmatively— and truthfully—but I'm afraid to. The fact that I am adopted is not a secret; Lori and I have always known we were adopted. There is never anything said about the women who gave birth to us or what happened to them. In my mind, my birth mother is a young woman, younger than Mom, with long hair she wears flipped up on the ends like Ann Marie on *That Girl*. In my fantasy, she was killed in a car accident along with her boyfriend, my birth father. I've never been told not to tell my friends I was adopted, but I sense that Mom and Dad would prefer I didn't. Stories about how Mom used to put a pillow under her coat before she went outside to shovel the driveway the winter before they got me and comments about how much I look like Mom have convinced me they want to keep up the illusion to the outside world that Lori and I are their real daughters.

I could lie and tell Dad I hadn't heard the conversation; then Dad wouldn't be able to get mad at me for telling Joan I was adopted, and the need for any further talk about adoption would be eliminated.

I choose the comfort and happiness of my dad over my little-girl desire to tell the truth. "No," I say, hopping off the piano bench and skipping back over to where Joan is pulling a brown knit dress onto my talking Barbie doll.

And with this simple one-word lie, I allow the illusion to continue. As I pick through the assortment of Barbie outfits strewn over the floor, I feel the familiar lump in my stomach begin to grow heavier and hotter.

Belonging

"There's a tomato coming!" Lori shouts. I, a big girl of eleven, know she means "tornado."

The hot, dry prairie wind is blowing hard, and it sparks our imaginations. We've heard stories about the tornado near Benson when Mom was a little girl. We know Mom and her family were at a picnic when they saw the funnel cloud touch down and head in the direction of the family farm. We've stood in the foundation of what remained of the house that the storm claimed. We know a baby was sleeping upstairs in the house when the tornado hit and that the baby was found alive some distance away when the storm passed.

"Let's run!" I call back to Lori, joining in on her game.

We race through the vacant lot next to Grandma's house toward Uncle Albert's big green garage, where Mom, Dad, Uncle Albert, Aunt Edie, and her husband, Uncle Bill, sit in lawn chairs, enjoying cold bottles of Pilsner. It's cooler in the garage, and there is more room there than in the tiny house where Grandma Sellsted raised her family.

A ruddy-faced bachelor, Uncle Albert has a bulbous nose and twinkling eyes and carries a chunk of something called snoose tucked inside his lower lip. I'm not sure what snoose is, but I know it comes out of a round, flat tin he always carries in his shirt pocket. It must not taste very good, because there is a dark mound of it in the corner of the outhouse where he spits it out. It's disgusting.

Sometimes Uncle Albert takes Lori and me with him when he is running errands. We go with him to nearby villages into wooden-floored stores, and we feel special when he introduces us as his nieces. We sit in the front of his big grain truck while it is being emptied at the elevator. We perch way up in the cab of his huge air-conditioned tractor when he works the farm. We go rock picking with him, and he teaches us how to chew grain to make gum.

Aunt Edie and Uncle Bill live in Stoughton, a village about eleven miles up the road from Benson. Aunt Edie's reddish hair and slender frame are a contrast to Mom's blonde hair and plump body, but their strikingly similar facial features leave no doubt that they are sisters. Lori and I adore our fun-loving, happy aunt. Dark-haired Uncle Bill works for the local co-op; he seems more serious than Aunt Edie and holds himself at a subtle distance from the rest of the family, but we love being with him, too.

Grandma Sellsted is sitting in the garage with a glass of juice; she has diabetes and can't drink beer like the rest of them. Sometimes Dad gives her a small glass of rye when he thinks no one is looking. Her eyes always light up when Dad is around. Grandma is a sharp woman with a bent back. She invariably wears nondescript cotton housedresses, heavy stockings, and utilitarian black shoes. Her white hair always looks the same, and her pinched, stern-looking face is testimony to years of struggle that seem to have hardened her. We have lots of pictures taken when I was a baby sitting on the laps of Aunt Edie, Uncle Albert, and Uncle Bill, but there are none of me sitting on Grandma's lap. I interpret that, coupled with her persistent "tsk-tsk" when I am around, as evidence of her disapproval.

Lori and I stumble breathlessly into the garage, and I sit down on the cement next to Aunt Edie's chair. She reaches out and rests her hand on my shoulder.

"What are you doing, kiddo?" she asks in her familiar, high-pitched voice.

"Nothing," I reply. "Just playing."

From her perch on Uncle Albert's knee, Lori pipes up, "We want a treat."

Uh oh, I think. Now she's going to get it. We're not supposed to ask for treats. I glance over at Dad and can tell he is just about to scold her, but Aunt Edie speaks first.

"Well, let's go for a walk then. Are you coming, Laura?" she says, turning toward Mom.

I can tell by Mom's face—her eyes aren't as clear as they usually are—that she is feeling the effects of the beer. The group has been sitting in the garage for much of the afternoon, and judging by the number of empty bottles on the floor, they have enjoyed more than just a few. I don't understand why people like Aunt Edie and Uncle Bill can drink beer and still act normal, but when Mom and Dad do, they get drunk.

Drunk: that's a bad word, one I'm not supposed to use. I'm not supposed to say "beer," either; we've been taught to call it "pop." But in the privacy of my thoughts, I call it what it is—beer. And Mom and Dad are drunk.

"No, I'll stay here, sis," Mom replies.

"Okay, come on, Skeezix," Aunt Edie says to Lori, who hops down from Uncle Albert's lap. "Let's go for a walk."

I love being in Benson, especially when Aunt Edie and Uncle Bill are here. I like to pretend that I am Mom and Lori is Aunt Edie when they were little girls. In my make-believe world, Mom is Grandma and Aunt Edie is Grandma's sister, Aunt Abby, who is my de facto grandma; she is large and cuddly, the opposite of Grandma in many ways. She lives in Estevan, and we see her less frequently than Grandma, but when we do she welcomes us and hugs us like I think a grandma should. I even call her "Grandma." Her love for Lori and me is confirmed in gifts of paper bags filled with crisp homemade gingersnaps and annual birthday cards that arrive in the mail with two-dollar bills tucked inside.

The three of us walk leisurely past the lilac hedge that borders Grandma's yard and out onto the dusty road in front. There is a forgotten wooden wagon wheel that fascinates me hidden in that hedge. I like to imagine the wagon it was once attached to and wonder which of my Sellsted ancestors owned it. We amble down the road toward the red one-room schoolhouse Mom and Aunt Edie once went to. Lori holds one of Aunt Edie's hands and chatters away. I have a plastic loop around my ankle, a new toy from Aunt Edie. Attached to the loop is a long plastic rope with a bell-shaped apparatus on the end. As I skip down the dusty road, the device on the end of the rope circles around me, and with my other foot, I lightly jump over it when it comes around.

Our little entourage turns left at the schoolhouse, and we step up onto a wooden sidewalk. There is a grain elevator next to the railroad track on the street behind Grandma's house, and across from the elevator are buildings that once served as a restaurant, a general store, and a post office. Aunt Abby once lived in the rooms behind the post office, and Aunt Edie was born there. All the stores have been closed and boarded up for years; the only one that's still open is the tiny corner store where Aunt Edie takes us to buy candy bars.

As we clop-clop along the wooden sidewalk, I imagine we are back in the days when the stores were open. The history of this little hamlet flows through our veins. Those who once lived here are part of us, and the stories we've heard about the past are part of us. That we were adopted is irrelevant. This is our family, and Benson is our history, too.

A Big Girl Now

I'm sitting on Mom and Dad's bed watching Mom get ready to go out for the evening. She's wearing a black chiffon cocktail dress with a full skirt, and she is digging around in her blue jewelry box.

"Don't go," I whine.

"We won't be gone too long," she says.

I don't believe her; I know Mom and Dad will stay out late, and when they come home, they will be acting funny because of the jungle juice they will have been drinking.

"But I'm scared." My throat hurts from holding back tears; I don't want to cry. Maybe if Mom realizes why I don't want her to go, she will change her mind.

"There is nothing to be afraid of," she says as she lifts a rhinestone broach out of her jewelry box and holds it up against her dress, checking out the look in her dresser mirror. "You're a big girl now."

It's already dark outside; maybe I would feel differently if it were still light, but I doubt it. I don't like the empty, lonely feeling that sits in the pit of my stomach like a lump of Plasticine when Mom and Dad go out. They've decided that now that I'm eleven, there's no need for Bev to come and babysit Lori and me anymore. They think I'm old enough to take care of Lori, but I don't feel old enough.

Lori and I used to have fun with Bev when she came—Bev, with her red hair and freckles and stacks of schoolbooks. It felt like a party when Bev was coming over. Mom would make a sandwich, wrap it in wax paper, and put it on a plate in the refrigerator next to a bottle of pop in case Bev got hungry. Lori would act goofy with excitement waiting for Dad's Oldsmobile to pull into the driveway with Bev inside. Usually Lori had to go to bed not long after Bev arrived, and Bev and I would sit together on the sofa, where she would show me the mysteries hidden in her schoolbooks. Some books had graphs and colored lines, and others had words I didn't recognize that Bev said were Latin.

Now Mom and Dad say we don't need to have Bev anymore.

"But Mom," I whine. "I don't want you to go. Please stay home." I can't help it. A tear sneaks out and slowly falls down my cheek.

"Linda," Mom says firmly, turning toward me while screwing on her rhinestone earrings. "We're going out, and you are going to be fine. You and Lori have stayed home before; there's nothing to be afraid of."

A sense of panic comes upon me, and my heart begins to beat faster. I know I should be happy that Mom thinks I'm a big girl, but I don't feel like a big girl; I feel like a very little girl who is being abandoned by her mommy.

Just then Lori comes running into the room and bounces up on the bed beside me. Dad follows behind with a glass of jungle juice in his hand.

"What's the matter, Lin?" Lori asks when she sees the lone tear on my cheek.

"Nothing." I'm the older sister; I should be the brave one.

Dad steps over to the dresser, picks up Mom's rhinestone necklace, drapes it around her neck, and fastens it in the back. It's the pretty necklace that looks like it's made of diamonds; sometimes I put it on my head and pretend I'm a princess with a tiara.

"Is something wrong, princess?" Dad asks.

"Come on, Lin," Lori says as she bounds off of the bed and runs toward the door. "Daddy said we can have some pop and chips!"

"Linda's fine," Mom tells Dad as she blots her freshly lipsticked mouth with tissue. "Aren't you, Linda?"

"Yes," I agree quietly, and Dad leaves to pour some pop for Lori.

Mom reaches into the top of her jewelry box, lifts out her gold heart necklace, and brings it over to me. It's a special necklace: Dad gave it to her when they got married in the big St. Andrew's church downtown.

"Here, sweetie," she says as she fastens it around my neck. "You can wear my locket for being such a big girl tonight, okay?"

I tuck Mom's locket on the inside of my flannel pajamas so Lori won't see it. If she does, she'll want Mom to give her something to wear, too, and if I'm going to be a big girl, then I deserve a reward just for myself.

Later, after Mom and Dad have gone, Lori lies sleeping in Dad's recliner and I sit on the brown sofa watching TV.

"*The FBI*, starring Efrem Zimbalist Jr.," the announcer says. Every Friday night we watch *The FBI*; usually I lie on the couch and fall asleep with my head in Mom's lap before it's over, but when they're not home, I try very hard to stay awake. "Also starring Phillip Abbott."

Suddenly the phone trills, startling me, and I run to the kitchen to pick it up before it wakes Lori up.

"Hi, kiddo!" It's my aunt calling.

"Aunt Edie!" I am always excited when she calls and I get to talk to her. This is the second reward for me tonight.

I tell her Mom and Dad are out, and by the time we finish talking, I feel better and stronger. I wonder if Aunt Edie thinks I'm big enough to stay home without Bev, but I don't ask her.

I tiptoe back into the living room where Lori is still fast asleep and settle back onto the couch. As *The FBI* continues, I reach into my pajama top, feeling for the locket. As I hold it in my hand, a sense of being special and loved by Mom comes over me.

Chameleon

Moose Jaw, Saskatchewan: the city with the funny name, the province with the unpronounceable name. Home. We live on the North Hill on Seventh Avenue in the bungalow Dad built shortly after he and Mom got married. I like hearing stories about how Dad built our house. I like looking at the blueprints when he brings them out and unrolls them for us to see; I'm proud of Dad.

When we go to the South Hill to visit Mom and Dad's friends or to watch a baseball game, we drive past the Robin Hood Flour Mill. On the side of the mill is a mural of a giant Robin Hood drawing his bow; that bow seems to follow us until we turn and lose sight of it.

Two blocks to the west is Elgin Park, where I play in the wading pool in the summertime, always careful—as Mom warns me every time—not to get my hair wet. I'm not sure why she tells me that; I think it's because she thinks I can't drown if my hair doesn't get wet.

Four blocks west is King George Elementary, a large two-story brick building that looks the same as many other schools in Moose Jaw. In fact, King Edward Elementary, the school Dad attended as a boy, is almost identical. A chain-link fence encloses two playgrounds on either side of the school—one for the boys and one for the girls. When it is time for us to go into school, one of the teachers stands at the top of the cement stairs in front and rings a hand bell, and we line up and wait for her to open the massive wooden doors.

Five blocks north is a hilly ravine we call the coulee, where we ride our bikes, explore, and let our imaginations take us on adventures. Six blocks south is the tall white house at 412 Moose Square where Dad grew up, and two blocks farther south is Graham Construction.

Dad goes to work every morning at Graham Construction, and Mom stays home with Lori and me. We grow up watching Granny Clampett ride into Beverly Hills perched atop a rocking chair in the back of a rickety truck on Saturday nights, and we wonder if Gilligan will ever get off of the island. Lori imagines herself as Zorro and leaves little pieces of paper with a *Z* on them all over the house. I, on the other hand, want to grow up to be like the cool and confident Mrs. Peel on *The Avengers.*

On the surface I have a happy and normal childhood.

Dad is strict and authoritarian, a slender man with characteristic German-Slavic cheekbones and thin lips, prone to unpredictable episodes of rage and periods of melancholy. His thinning, graying hair makes him look even more than eleven years older than Mom. There's a story about how once, when I was a baby and Mom and Dad were in a restaurant with me, a stranger said how nice it was to see a grandfather out with his daughter and granddaughter. Dad was never amused by that story. In later years, when I see the movie *On Golden Pond,* I am struck by how much Henry Fonda's character reminds me of Dad. Yet despite his stern exterior, Dad has a tender heart for his three blondes; I am his "princess," Lori is his "angel," and Mom is his "queen."

Mom is a short, soft, roundish woman with an easygoing, fun-loving nature. She wears lipstick during the day and is always neatly attired in cotton dresses in the summer and slacks and blouses in the winter. She has friends over for tea some afternoons and brings out her Royal Albert American Beauty china to serve homemade peanut butter cookies and matrimonial squares.

Lori and I share a bedroom. We have matching twin beds with pink ballerina bedspreads and a nine-drawer dresser that is a source of conflict whenever we try to divide the space evenly between us. We put masking tape on the floor or string yarn from wall to wall to mark our territory in the bedroom, but no arrangement works out very well. One of us always ends up with no way in or out of her space without trespassing on the other's, and the battle is on again. Dad halfheartedly threatens to buy us boxing gloves so we can duke out our conflicts. We frequently yell and call each other names, but our conflicts never turn physical.

Our front yard is surrounded by the quintessential white picket fence. There is a long cement driveway at the side of the house, leading to the garage where Dad parks his Oldsmobile, which he calls his "iron horse." In the winter he turns the driveway into a skating rink for Lori and me.

The backyard is a grassy and private refuge from the oppressive heat of the house in summer. Mom cooks hamburgers on the barbecue, Lori and I roast marshmallows, and Mom and Dad enjoy cold bottles of Pilsner beer. One side of the yard is lined with lilac and honeysuckle bushes, and Mom's tall, pink gladiolas grow along the back fence. In the back corner is a maple tree with a branch that's just right for perching on when I want to be alone. I sit up in the tree and feel safe, secure, and invisible.

Our neighborhood is safe; we have the run of it, and we know all the neighbors. At one end of the street is the IGA grocery store that Mom sends me to when she needs some ingredient for lunch or supper. I repeat what she wants over and over in my mind all the way there so I won't forget. I still hear myself chant "six slices of mac-and-cheese, please" whenever I see cold cuts in a deli case.

There is a Church of the Nazarene on the side of our house where our bedrooms are, and on Sunday nights in summer, when our windows are open, I fall asleep to the sound of piano music. At the other end of the street is the Minto United Church, which we attend sporadically. I sing in the children's choir and attend Brownie meetings in the Christian Education Center attached to the church.

Every Saturday morning, Dad gives me two quarters for my allowance, and with great ceremony I deposit the quarters in a heavy glass globe that serves as my savings bank. I resent that glass globe for taking my allow-ance—for my education, Mom and Dad insist. It means nothing to a little girl who just wants to go down the street to Tom's Candy Store, and I don't understand why they give me something I can't keep.

I spend hours sitting on the polished hardwood floor in front of a book-case, poring over gray volumes of the *Book of Popular Science,* blue and red volumes of the encyclopedia *Canadiana,* and the burgundy set of *Richards Topical Encyclopedia.* The bookcase is right outside the living room, where Mom and Dad spend much of the weekend sitting with glasses of rye and water or bottles of beer, smoking cigarettes and talking. Sometimes I wonder what they find to talk about hour after hour, but the amber-colored jungle juice they drink seems to keep the conversation flowing.

I hate how the alcohol seems to rob me of my parents; I fantasize that if my birth parents or the adoption agency knew about my parents' drinking, they would come and get me.

By the time Sunday evening comes around the alcohol has run out, things usually start to get back to normal. We gather in the front room to watch *Walt Disney.* Sometimes Dad makes cinnamon toast, and I start to relax again. Other times, I hear Mom call Graham Construction on Monday morning and say Dad is sick and can't come into work. Then I know the binge is likely to last all week, and I go to school with a hot lump of shame in my stomach.

As much as I love Mom and Dad, I'm plagued by the feeling that I'm somewhere I don't belong. But like a chameleon, I blend in and adapt. Sometimes I am joined in my imagination by two sisters—we are a set of triplets. Belinda is the strong one; she has opinions and preferences and is, in a sense, my protector. Melinda is quiet like me, but her heart is purer than mine; she is like Beth in *Little Women*—pure of heart and gentle in spirit. Sometimes they join me when I am walking to Mrs. Knight's house for piano lessons after school. In my imagination we talk about our day at school. With them beside of me, I feel safe, strong, and good—complete. They never stay long, and I am always sad when they leave.

The irony is that there really are three of me—three selves—though I don't realize it at the time. There is Linda the adoptee, trying to fit in where I don't feel I belong. I tread softly, making sure I'm not too visible and feeling like a guest wherever I am. There's the girl I would be if I weren't adopted—if I had stayed with my birth mother and grown up surrounded by extended family who looked like me, who had similar mannerisms and character traits—and that's Belinda. Finally, there's Melinda, the one who would be Mom and Dad's biological child. She would be complete and transparent, untainted with the inner shame I carry at my core.

My self is fractured, and I'm not sure who I am or where I fit.

Heritage

"What are you?"

It is a common question among my elementary-school friends. Perhaps it's prompted by a history lesson about life in the settlement of Canada. Perhaps it's a reflection of the common human desire to know one another better by understanding where we each come from. Or maybe it's an expression of the innate sense that we have to know who our own people are in order to understand who we ourselves are.

My next-door neighbor Susan is Ukrainian; she calls her grandparents Baba and Gido. My school friend Nona is English, and I'm sometimes jealous of the close relationship she has with her cousins.

Everyone has their answers down pat, their family history handed down by osmosis in the stories told by parents and grandparents. "If only I could make borscht the way Great-Aunt Charlotte did back in the old country," or "This little doll belonged to your Great-Grandma Sabina when she was a little girl in Holland."

I've heard family stories, too. I know that my German paternal grandfather, Louis Adolph Brauer, who died when I was five, was ashamed of his middle name. I've seen pictures of my great-grandparents' fiftieth-anniversary celebration. They were the first in the family to come across the ocean. Dad was a little boy at the time of the anniversary celebration and served as ring bearer when they renewed their wedding vows in the middle of a North Dakota field.

There are fewer stories about my Norwegian maternal ancestors. I've heard about "the Graves boys," my Grandma Sellsted's brothers, who were killed within a few months of each other in World War I. Mom's heritage pops out when she utters her own version of the traditional Norwegian expression of surprise, exhaustion, or dismay, but instead of *uff-da* she gives it a twist of her own that is more like *uff-da boof-da*. And so, having heard these stories often, it is natural for me to respond that I am German and Norwegian.

When we study the science of genetics and are tasked with drawing our family tree to demonstrate how traits like eye and hair color are passed on, I naturally draw boxes to represent members of my German and Norwegian family. In addition to Mom and Dad, I draw boxes for Aunt Edie, Uncle Bill, Uncle Albert, all of Dad's sisters, my grandparents—Tenor and Isabelle Sellsted and Louis and Helena Brauer—and their parents, my great-grandparents. All the dominant and recessive traits I learn about in class fall neatly into place, thanks to the deliberate matching of Mom and Dad with the physical characteristics of my birth parents.

I understand that even though I'm a well-behaved, honest, obedient, good student, it is okay to perpetuate the lie of my heritage. It is okay to pretend I am German and Norwegian and that the family tree I draw is mine. In fact, it is more than okay—it is expected. To do anything else is unimaginable. I learn to speak something that I know isn't true as if it is and at some level convince myself that it is fact. I learn to ignore the ache of deception in the pit of my stomach.

Keeping Secrets

$\mathcal{W}$e're having Christmas at Aunt Edie and Uncle Bill's house. I've never been with them on Christmas before and I'm excited. Aunt Edie's Christmas tree is different from the one we always have; it's shorter and wider than our real tree, and it doesn't have the same pine scent that conjures up Christmases past and future. It doesn't even pretend to be a real tree—it's silver—but I like it. I'm fascinated by the colored lights on the silver boughs, that have a liquid that bubbles when they're turned on. They're neat.

Lori and I are settled in the sofa bed in the spare room. Mom and Dad, Aunt Edie and Uncle Bill, and their friends, Lionel and Cora, are having drinks in the living room. We were allowed to stay up late and have potato chips, sausage, crackers, and Coca-Cola with the adults, but it's late now, and their voices have gotten louder throughout the evening. I was happy to head off to the sanctuary of the guest room when Mom said it was time.

Aunt Edie's friend is named Cora, but Aunt Edie and Mom call her "Mercy" when she isn't around because she has a habit of shrieking "mercy!" when she is excited about something she's talking about. I think Cora is Aunt Edie's best friend next to my mom. I don't like Cora's husband, Lionel, because I don't think he likes my dad. I sense an alliance between Lionel and Uncle Bill that doesn't include my dad, kind of like the way some kids at school play together all the time and don't invite me to join them. They're nice to me, but it's understood by all of us that I'm not really part of their group.

That's what I sense between Lionel and Dad, and it bothers me. Like last night, when we were all over at Lionel and Cora's house, and Lionel was showing off his new hi-fi system. He bragged about how the music we heard came from the reels of magnetic tape, and Uncle Bill enthusiastically agreed that the system produced the best music he had ever heard. Dad listened politely to their conversation about pickup arms and tweeters, but I knew he didn't really understand what they were talking about, just like I knew Lionel and Uncle Bill knew it too.

We have a record player inside a cabinet at home; it's old and doesn't have any extra speakers attached to it, like Lionel has for his hi-fi. We use our record player all the time to listen to Dean Martin or Patsy Cline on big $33\frac{1}{3}$ albums, and Lori and I even have our own Christmas record. Sometimes on the weekend, Dad puts on a stack of heavy records he calls 78s. The music they play is scratchy, but I like some of the silly songs, like "Rubber Dolly" and "I'm My Own Grandpa." Our record player is good enough for us; we don't need a fancy hi-fi like Lionel's.

Lionel and Cora have a handful of kids; I'm not sure exactly how many because some of them are grown up and aren't around much when we're there. But they have a little girl named Myra, who is around the same age as Lori and me. We play with her sometimes when we we're in Stoughton. She spends a lot of time at Aunt Edie and Uncle Bill's house; she sleeps over so often that Cora and Lionel make jokes about how Aunt Edie and Uncle Bill have adopted her. They haven't really, even though they have a picture of her on top of their TV set, along with her bronzed baby shoes. They just like having her around because they don't have any kids of their own. Myra, for her part, loves my aunt and uncle like second parents. Sometimes Lori gets mad at Myra when we are playing with her; I think she feels jealous of all the time Myra gets to spend with Aunt Edie. Sometimes I do too, but I never let on.

I lay awake on the sofa bed listening to the laughter in the living room and Cora's exclamations of "mercy!" While Lori snores softly next to me, I imagine what I might find under the Christmas tree in the morning. There are identical boxes with Lori's name and my name on them; I suspect they're matching dolls. I wish people would stop giving us matching things, but I guess matching dolls are better than matching clothes. We've got way too many of those.

I must have fallen asleep, because suddenly I am startled awake.

"Bill! Leave him alone!" I hear Aunt Edie's shrill voice shriek from the other room.

I toss back the covers gently so as not to wake Lori and tiptoe to the bedroom door, which is partially open. I peek through the crack in the door and see Dad and Uncle Bill in the dining room surrounded by Mom, Aunt Edie, Lionel, and Cora. Uncle Bill's hands are around my dad's neck, and he is shaking so hard that Dad's head is wobbling back and forth. My stomach twists into knots as I watch Mom and Aunt Edie take hold of Uncle Bill's arms and attempt to pull him away from Dad.

Uncle Bill releases his grip, and Dad stumbles backward. Lionel steps forward and takes Uncle Bill by the shoulder, and together they walk back into the living room. I quietly close the door of the guest room and crawl back into bed next to a still-sleeping Lori so no one will know I saw what happened.

The next morning the commotion of the previous night seems to be forgotten, and I begin to wonder if I dreamed the whole thing. Lionel and Cora are gone, and everyone sits around in their pajamas in the living room, the adults sipping mugs of milky coffee while Lori and I open our presents. The two big boxes contain matching dolls, just as I suspected. I don't know what to make of what I saw the night before and don't say anything about it. It's easy for me to keep secrets; secrecy is becoming normal in my life.

Adoptee Adolescence

Adoptees are handicapped in accomplishing virtually all the tasks of adolescence. Because they lack the basic knowledge of their biological roots, they have a harder time trying to form their own sense of identity.

—JOE SOLL, *ADOPTION HEALING*

Turning Point

*I*t's October 31, and I hurry home from school in anticipation of the evening to come; at eleven years old, I know it will probably be my last year of trick-or-treating. This year Mom didn't take even me shopping for a costume, and that's just fine with me. I hate those plastic masks with eye holes that are too small to see out of and the little cutout of a mouth that doesn't allow enough air to get out and makes my face sweat inside the mask despite the frigid Saskatchewan air outside. The costumes are all the same: a plastic robe-like garment large enough to fit over my winter coat and adorned with the appropriate décor to make it look like a witch's dress or a superhero's costume. And that mask.

This year I have my own plan. I am going to dress up like Aunt Jemima, the woman on the bottle of pancake syrup. Since we always have to wear our costumes over our winter coats, I've decided to put on an old dress of Mom's, wrap a scarf around my head (which will help keep me warm), and paint my face with a concoction of cocoa and water. In previous years, I've seen others dressed up this way, but no one ever told me that the cocoa was supposed to be mixed with cold cream and not water. That's a lesson I'll learn before the evening is over.

As I run across the lawn toward the side door, I am surprised to see Dad's white Oldsmobile parked in the driveway. He doesn't usually get home before me. I kick off my shoes and bound up the two steps into the kitchen. My eyes immediately focus on the kitchen table, where two glasses of rye and water sit in front of Mom and Dad as they talk quietly. My stomach lurches at the sight of the alcohol, and when I look up at my parents' faces, I realize something bad has happened.

Dad has lost his job at Graham Construction.

I'm annoyed that Mom isn't making supper yet; usually on Halloween we eat early so Lori and I can go out before it gets too late. I'm even more annoyed that Mom and Dad are drinking. I don't understand the implications of Dad losing his job, and as I smear the cocoa and water mixture on my face, I resolve not to let that spoil my evening. Mom gives Lori and me sandwiches, and we head out for some fun.

When we return home, our plastic jack-o-lanterns filled with candy and my face burning from the cracked and dried cocoa, Mom and Dad are still at the kitchen table talking about what they will do now.

———◆———

Dad collects unemployment insurance. As months go by and he still can't find a new job, Mom takes a job at a bakery. Dad expands the scope of his search, and after about four months, he lands a job with a credit union in a small town in British Columbia. He and Mom fell in love with the beauty of the mountains there on a vacation when I was a baby. They're optimistic about moving. Dad takes our Scamper travel-trailer and leaves for BC, and Lori and I stay with Mom in Moose Jaw to pack and wait until our house is sold.

I remember this summer, my twelfth, as one of the best of my childhood.

Mom works all day at the bakery, and I look after Lori, keep the house tidy, and make sure the lawns are watered. Mom enrolls Lori in a couple of activities, so in the morning, the two of us set off on our bikes to the ball field for baseball camp or up to the high school for the gymnastics program. Though we're separated by only two and a half years, the age gap between us seems wider. There is never a question of us spending time together in the afternoon; we have little in common.

After a lunch of canned spaghetti, she usually heads off to play with her friends, and I grab a library book and head downstairs to the back bedroom, the coolest part of the house. I'm finally allowed to tap into the despised glass globe full of quarters, and I calculate that I have enough money to buy an orange Creamsicle or an ice-cream sandwich from Tom's corner store every afternoon for the entire summer.

The Bookmobile comes to the parking lot of the IGA every couple of weeks, and I carefully choose new books. I love the solitude and routine of those summer afternoons. I read countless books, write letters to Dad, and enjoy the peace and quiet.

Near the end of summer, our house sells, and Mom makes plans for us to join Dad in BC. In the final weeks before we are to leave, I take solitary walks and try to engrave images of Moose Jaw in my mind to carry with me. I imagine a voice narrating my life saying, "She would never forget the Palm Dairy (or Central Collegiate or Joiners Store) for as long as she lived." I try not to cry; I'm looking forward to having our family together again, but I'm silently grieving the loss of all that is familiar and secure in my life.

One day Mom asks if I've called any of my friends to tell them we're moving. It hasn't occurred to me to say good-bye to the friends I've known since kindergarten, and it certainly hasn't occurred to me that any of them might want to bid me farewell. I am more upset about leaving the place than the people.

All too soon our last night in Moose Jaw arrives. Our furniture has been taken away in the orange Allied Van Line truck, and Mom's little Ford Falcon has been loaded onto a car transporter and taken away. Mom, Lori, and I stand on the landing of our empty house, looking out the window of the side door and watching for the taxi that will take us to the Greyhound bus station.

Mom is cross with Lori, who is bawling dramatically at the thought of leaving, and while her attention is diverted, I step quietly up the two steps that lead to the empty kitchen to say a silent farewell to the house that Dad built. The soles of my sneakers are silent on the hardwood floors as I step out of the kitchen and into the hall. At the door of each room, I stand for a moment, slowing casting my gaze around the perimeter, trying to drink in the images. My throat hurts from holding back tears, but I am determined to be strong.

Sudden activity on the landing draws me back to the present. Lori calls, "Lin! It's here!" and Mom hustles to get our luggage out the door so as not to keep the taxi waiting.

We are off on a journey to a new life.

Alienated and Alone

*I*t's after midnight when the whish of the airbrakes whispers to the sleeping passengers that the bus has arrived at its destination: Princeton, British Columbia. I crane my neck toward the window, looking for Dad. The bus pulls into the parking spot, hissing and groaning to a stop. The door opens, and there's a smell of diesel. Dad is standing on the sidewalk, smiling and waving, but I see something familiar and disappointing in his eyes.

I climb down the last step of the bus behind Lori, and Dad approaches us for a welcoming hug. I'm on high alert when I smell alcohol and notice his slightly unsteady stance. I glance over at Mom to see her reaction to this boozy welcome. She just looks weary.

We stay in our camper trailer at a campground next to the Similkameen River while Mom and Dad look for a house. Lori and I explore the area around the campground; for two prairie girls, the hills and rivers of British Columbia are new and exciting. We walk along the stony bank of the river, inhaling the dank smell that is like nothing we have smelled before. We hike up surrounding hills and run among tall, craggy pine trees on soft paths carpeted with fallen needles that release a pine aroma with each step we take. We explore the benches and flats of Princeton and are surprised to find wooden fences built in a zigzag fashion leading down the side of a hill toward the center of the village.

Mom and Dad rent a small bungalow. In typical Lori fashion, my sister makes many friends in the neighborhood easily and quickly before school starts in September. I am thankful there is a girl my age living next door, and Danna and I become fast friends.

Everything about our life seems different in Princeton, and I struggle to adjust to living in what feels like a foreign land. The cliques in the village were formed generations ago. With no familial ties to anyone, we are on the outside from the beginning. I miss the familiarity of our home and neighborhood in Moose Jaw. I miss Aunt Edie and Uncle Bill and Uncle Albert.

Mom and Dad find their new social circle by spending time at the Royal Canadian Legion, the Elks Club, and the local hotel bar. They start bringing new acquaintances home. Mom's American Beauty china is relegated to the new corner china cabinet she orders from the Sears catalog; she no longer uses it to serve tea and squares to friends in the afternoon. The new crowd that shows up on the weekend expects drinks, and if there is food served, it's Ritz Crackers, cheese, garlic sausage, and pickles.

The first time it happens I am playing the piano. The house is smaller than our house in Moose Jaw, and we've had to be creative with where to put everything, so the piano is in my bedroom. Mom and Dad are busy doing something in the living room or the kitchen. One of my parents' friends—his name is Bob—comes into the bedroom. I don't know why. He sits down next to me on the piano bench, reaches over, and touches me in that most private of places. I freeze and try to ignore his unwelcome touch. After a moment he removes his hand and wordlessly gets up and leaves the room to join my parents. I don't consider telling Mom and Dad what he did. It isn't a big deal, and the uncomfortable feeling I get in my stomach isn't much different from the feeling of shame I always carry with me anyway.

One night I am asleep in my bedroom while my parents entertain friends in the living room. I awaken to find another of their friends—Harry—sitting on the side of my bed.

Dad storms into the room and booms, "Harry! What the hell are you doing in here? Get out of here!"

Harry leaves my room, Dad closes my bedroom door, and the incident is never spoken of. The worst part is that Mom and Dad continue to socialize with the man. I feel betrayed and unprotected and am convinced I made the right decision in not telling them about the earlier incident.

Over the next few years, there are other incidents that I brush off and tell no one about, stuffing down the discomfort I feel. A feeling of shame has always been at the core of me, so it feels oddly normal to have this new sense of shame enter my life. I'm on the cusp of adolescence, and without anything to counteract the attachment of shame to sex, the two become firmly linked in my mind.

———◆———

I am most comfortable with the academic crowd at school. I am already a year younger than my classmates, as I was in an accelerated program in Moose Jaw. After the first couple of months, the school contacts my parents to discuss the possibility of putting me ahead another year. Mom and Dad refuse to let them, fearing I will have trouble fitting in with my classmates if I am so much younger than they are. They needn't have worried; I feel alienated and alone anyway, as if I'm looking at the world from behind an invisible shield. At times I can almost hear a whir as it descends around me, keeping me separate and safe. It is as if I've been adopted all over again into a community of people that isn't my own. I long for King George School and the friends I left behind without bidding them farewell.

I often retreat to my room to write poetry or stories on the manual typewriter Dad gives me. There is something about the sensation of my fingers on the typewriter keys that allows my mind to enter a place of peace, where I can leave behind the expectations of others and be the person I was meant to be. My thoughts and feelings flow out through my fingers as they fly over the typewriter keys and turn into something tangible in the form a written word on a sheet of yellow newsprint.

One day I share one of my poems with Dad.

"Why are you so sad?" he asks me after he finishes it.

I am pleased that he sees through the words on the page but embarrassed to have him see a vulnerable part of me.

"I'm not sad," I reassure him. But I am, and I become even sadder when he probes no further.

I feel the need to be reassured of Mom's love.

"Do you love me?" I ask her repeatedly.

I know she does but I need to hear the words.

At night, in the dark solitude of my bedroom, I weep. I cry deep and heaving sobs into my pillow, overwhelmed by a grief I can't explain.

Idiopathic Scoliosis

*I*know there is a problem long before the X-ray confirms it and reveals my secret. Like most sixteen-year-old girls, I want to fit in and look like my friends, but I've known for some time that something is different about the way my body is changing. It starts gradually, with my clothes not quite fitting the same. In time, I notice a visible change in the height of my shoulders and hips and realize that one side of my waist curves in while the other stays almost straight. I begin wearing oversized shirts to hide the asymmetry, and this allows me to keep these changes secret for a time. But when another visit to the doctor for chronic stomach aches prompts an X-ray of my torso, my secret is out, and I am referred to an orthopedic surgeon in Vancouver, BC.

A few weeks later, I sit in Dr. Tredwell's office with Mom and Dad, watching as he draws lines on the X-ray that he has snapped onto a light box and calculates the degree to which my spine is curved. He explains that the condition is called idiopathic scoliosis, which simply means "a curvature of the spine of unknown origin."

"It runs in families," he says. "Is there anyone else in your family who seems to have a twisted or hunched back?"

Mom and Dad respond negatively. The fact that I am adopted is not mentioned.

Dr. Tredwell recommends surgery to insert a Harrington rod in my spine; he says the curve will continue to worsen without treatment. After surgery, he explains, I will be wrapped in a full-body cast to protect my spine during the many months of healing. I will spend four months in a full-body cast, during which time I will be confined to bed, followed by two months in a lighter body cast.

By the time we leave his office we have a date set for the operation, and I am astonished at how quickly my life has changed. As soon as I finish eleventh grade, I will return to Vancouver for the surgery; I'll miss much of my senior year.

As Dad pulls out into the busy city traffic, I sit in the backseat, unsuccessfully trying to hold back tears. Dad glances in the rearview mirror just as I'm wiping my eyes.

"What's wrong?" he asks

I could say I'm disappointed at being robbed of my senior year. I could say I'm afraid of having major surgery. I could ask why they didn't tell the doctor I'm adopted. Instead I mutter, "Nothing," and turn to look out the window, still fighting not to cry.

In retrospect, I marvel at Dad's question. It should have been obvious that the surgeon's news was upsetting to me and that I needed to talk about it and be reassured that everything would turn out all right. But that isn't the way of our family. Don't talk, don't trust, don't feel: that is our way.

In June we travel back to Vancouver, and I am admitted to hospital to prepare for the surgery. I spend most of the first two weeks in bed, attached to pulleys and weights that stretch my back. My hips ache from the constant pull of the traction. Mom and Dad return home, and I am left alone and lonely as I wait for the traction to stretch my spine enough to make me ready for surgery.

Despite my loneliness, a new side of me emerges during those first weeks. This is the first time I'm on my own and away from the watchful eyes of my parents, the first time I've felt free to be something other than what they expect of me. During the hours when I'm not in traction, I mingle with other young people in the common areas of the ward. The nurses introduce me to others who also have scoliosis: Ron, whose curve is much worse than mine and who has just had his surgery, and Nancy, who has been through surgery and the long months of wearing a body cast and has just had her final cast removed. Nancy and I visit Ron in his room and we talk about how we feel. Nancy helps us understand what lies ahead. I get to know a young man named David, who has recently lost an arm in a motorcycle accident. The two of us spend a lot of time talking together; there is a touch of flirtation in our conversations. He's safe, we're in a hospital, and I'll probably never see him again.

All too soon these days are over, and the day of my surgery arrives.

———

After the operation, I wake on a narrow bed called a Stryker frame—a stretcher just wide enough for my body with armrest attachments on each side. The stretcher is attached to a frame that allows it to be rotated 360 degrees. Every few hours, the nurses place a second stretcher on top of me, place my arms by my side, and strap me into the contraption. Then, in one swift movement, they flip me 180 degrees so I am either staring down at the floor or up at the ceiling.

I learn new ways of doing everyday tasks as I lie on my back or stomach, able to move only my arms. One of the biggest challenges is learning to eat a meal while lying flat on my back. The nurses adjust a standing mirror beside my bed, which lets me see the reflection of a plate of food they place upon my chest. I get to be pretty good at using the mirror to pick up larger pieces of food but am never happy to see peas on my plate.

Mom and Dad visit on the weekends, bringing treats like German chocolate cake. On one visit I request some new books to read: *Once is Not Enough* by Jacqueline Susann and *Fear of Flying* by Erica Jong. Mom is concerned enough about the title of *Once is Not Enough* to ask what it is about, but *Fear of Flying* makes it past her radar. I'm happy to escape into the adult worlds portrayed in these books. They're a welcome change from the gothic mysteries of Mom's that I've been reading, even if they are pretty racy reading for a seventeen-year-old.

As my back heals and grows stronger, something in my character begins to grow stronger too. A new self-confidence comes over me, a sense of independence, which seems odd, since I am trapped in the Stryker frame. But during this time I don't feel I have to act *as if* anymore—*as if* I fit where I don't feel I do; *as if* I am someone I'm not. I'm free to be me or at least the person I believe to be me at the time.

After three weeks in the Stryker frame, my back is healed enough to allow the doctor to apply the full-body cast and move me to a regular hospital bed. I am still unable to sit up or get out of bed, but it's the first step toward going home, and I'm delighted. After a few days, the cast is dry enough for me to leave the hospital, and I am transported home to Princeton.

I'm confined to bed for the next four months, and I have no choice but to allow others to care for me. It's a nightmare to deal with the loss of my independence; even toileting is no longer private, and I'm forced to deal with the indignity of having someone else care for me in that way. My friend, Danna, visits often and tells me about the plans for the upcoming graduation celebration. She fills me in on who is dating whom and entertains me with dramatic stories about her and her boyfriend. The young man I had been casually seeing during eleventh grade stops by now and then. Sometimes he sits in the chair next to my bed and watches TV with me for a while.

I've enrolled in correspondence classes so I don't fall behind in schoolwork, and one of the unexpected benefits is that I am able to take writing and literature classes not offered at my school. I spend many lonely days, while Mom and Dad are at work and Lori is at school, working on my assignments and nourishing my passion for writing. It's not all bad; I've long been comfortable with solitude. It's harder now, though, as I feel like I'm being left behind while life for my friends carries on.

In late November I am transported back to the hospital, and the heavy body cast is replaced by the lighter-weight walking cast. I am delighted to have a measure of freedom and the chance to catch up with my friends and move back into my social circle.

Finally, in February, seven months after my ordeal began, the time comes to emerge from my plaster cocoon, and I'm pleased to find a body I can learn to love. It isn't perfect; some of the spinal curvature will always remain. But I'm thankful for the obvious improvement and confident that I'll be able to hide what's left of the curve with carefully chosen clothing. It's just another secret to keep.

Near the end of my senior year, I return to school. Plans are in full swing for pre-grad parties, the graduation ceremony, after-grad parties, the yearbook, and other senior activities. Everyone tries to make me feel included, but having missed a good part of the planning, I feel detached from the preparations and the graduation itself. Even more, I feel like a fraud on graduation day when I walk across the stage wearing my blue formal gown to accept the scroll of paper handed to each graduate that symbolizes the high school diploma we will receive in the mail later. I did not complete all of my correspondence classes and will not be receiving a graduation diploma in the mail.

A Life of My Own

This sense of a terrifying free-fall through the universe is a consequence of adoptees' not feeling rooted in their own factual being and history. They feel a fundamental disconnection from themselves and those around them, which they describe as feeling as if they are in a fog, weightless, floating above the Earth.

—BETTY JEAN LIFTON, *JOURNEY OF THE ADOPTED SELF*

Once an Adoptee...

February 2009

What I've only recently come to understand is that leaving Saskatchewan triggered deep feelings of loss and abandonment within me. Saskatchewan was the only home I had ever known, my *mother*land, if you will. I knew I was born in Regina. I had grown up in Moose Jaw. Everything familiar and comforting to me was there, and just when I was on the cusp of adolescence, it was all taken away.

I rejected Princeton unconsciously from the beginning to protect myself from attaching and risking further loss. Of course at the time, all I knew was that I was in unfamiliar territory and needed to protect myself from harm. The walls of protection that distanced me from other people went up quickly and naturally.

If you had asked me at the time if I was affected by being an adoptee, I would have responded negatively and told you I rarely thought about it. But the wounds were there, even if they didn't show. In fact, it's only in recent years that my response to that question changed; I know better now. Once an adoptee, always an adoptee, and when we least expect it, we're reminded that we are forever branded with a big *A* for Adoptee.

A few months after my fiftieth-birthday milestone, it's time for another marker of the passing of time: the annual mammogram. I schedule it for first thing in the morning and arrive early, trying not to work myself into a sweat because I'm not supposed to apply deodorant.

I wait in front of the mammogram machine while the technician prepares at her computer. My breasts will be tucked and flattened between two metal plates, and I will lean in to ensure the fullest compression, the firmest pressure, so the equipment can detect any tumors lurking deep inside my breasts. I give in to the momentary discomfort for the greater good of knowing I'm healthy.

The greatest discomfort comes when the technician asks the question I've been dreading.

"Do you have any family history of breast cancer?"

Every year I chide myself: I should have planned for this and prepared my answer in advance. The way I answer changes from year to year, depending on the explanation I feel up to providing each time.

"I don't know. I'm adopted," is simplest, but it's not entirely true, and truth is important to me.

The truth is that I've recently learned I have a sister who has breast cancer, and I don't know if she has finished chemotherapy or if she will have radiation, or how she is feeling, or what her long-term prognosis is. Women who have a sister with breast cancer are supposed to visit her, take her gifts, make her a quilt, get involved with breast-cancer awareness and fund-raising, wear a pink ribbon. I, the faux sister, have done none of these things save for the pink ribbon I wear on the security badge I take to work every day.

On this day I decide to honor my sister: "My sister is battling breast cancer right now."

"Oh, I am so sorry," the technician responds predictably. "Are there any other members of your family who have had breast cancer?"

I take a deep breath and in the brief moment between my inhalation and exhalation make a choice between the long answer and the short answer.

"No, she is the only one."

Show Me the Way

*I*t is 1977, almost one year after my high school graduation, and Peter Frampton is begging for someone to "Show Me the Way" on his classic *Frampton Comes Alive!* album. I am eighteen and appear confident; for the most part, I've managed to stuff down and ignore the part of me that feels unworthy and unlovable. I have the rest of my life stretching out in front of me and am pretty sure I know the way and could show Mr. Frampton if he cared to ask me.

I am working at the Similkameen Mine as a keypunch operator. The pay is relatively good for someone with no post-secondary education and no experience, and I have more money than I know what to do with. I long for independence and fantasize about an apartment of my own like Mary Tyler Moore's on TV, but Mom and Dad convince me I can't afford to move out. I can't help but wonder how my friends have managed to break away and get places of their own, but I don't challenge the status quo.

I save enough to make a down payment on a brand-new car—a metallic-blue Dodge Arrow. I go to parties. I live for the moment. When Danna comes home from a semester at university, I listen to her stories with a twinge of envy, but the idea of attending college seems out of reach for me because of the academic stumble that prevented me from getting my high school diploma. I know I want to be a writer, but when I reveal my dream, the general response is that one can't make a living by writing. That discourages me from going to university; there's nothing else I care about enough to study. I continue to peck away at my typewriter, turning out poetry and stories, and I read literary journals like *The Malahat Review* and *Writer's Digest*. I even submit some pieces and begin collecting the requisite rejection letters.

One evening in February, Danna and I and a couple of other girlfriends go out for an evening at the Elks Club. None of us are over the legal drinking age, but identification is rarely asked for. In fact, I've periodically enjoyed drinks at the Elks Club since a boyfriend took me there when I was fifteen.

I am wearing a tight-fitting T-shirt with a picture of Freddie Prinze in *Chico and the Man* over baggy, high-waisted jeans and brown-heeled loafers we call "shit-kickers." My blonde hair hangs long and straight, and, with my straightened spine and new contact lenses, I appear to be a confident young woman.

The room is darkened, and though none of us are smokers, blue, smoky air swirls around the table where the four of us are talking and laughing over Bloody Caesars. Someone has plugged the jukebox at the back of the room with quarters, and as Marie Osmond begins to sing "Paper Roses," a good-looking, dark-haired man swaggers over and invites me to dance. I'm flattered by the attention.

"Well, I'll have to think about it," I respond coyly.

I have no intention of dancing with him; I am enjoying the evening with my girlfriends, but I don't know how to turn him down flat. I expect him to return to his own table but instead this seemingly self-assured man pulls out the chair next to me, sits down, and allows a moment to pass.

"Well, have you thought about it yet?"

His unexpected behavior breaks the ice, and laughing, I agree to a dance.

I can't know this is a watershed moment that will change the course of the rest of my life.

Later, after all but Danna and I have called it a night, we join the table he is sharing with his friends and continue drinking and dancing. I learn his name is Ken, he's married with three children, works at the mine during the week, returns home to his family on the weekends, and is sixteen years older than me. I'm attracted to him; he's good-looking, and his attention makes me feel charming and desirable. When the evening is over, swept away by his flattery and with my judgment clouded by the alcohol, I go back to his hotel and spend the night with him.

It's my first time, and the next day I feel different, as though I've closed the door on my innocence and opened the door to a darker part of myself.

From that night on, Ken and I see each other regularly. That he is in town during the week, unencumbered by a wife or children, allows me to overlook the fact that he's a married man. I'm ashamed of what I am doing; I know it's wrong, but the shame isn't enough to make me stop. Having Ken in my life fills a void. It gives me an identity I don't have without him. I don't know who I am on my own and can easily accept his opinions, likes, and dislikes as if they are mine. It's not much different from how I adapted as a child.

Soon he stops going home on the weekends, and we start spending time together in the nearby town of Penticton, where we dine at good restaurants and dance the night away at the discos. I like that he's choosing me to the exclusion of someone else. I like that I'm living an adult life. I like that being with him is giving me the strength to move out of Mom and Dad's house and start a life of my own.

Motherhood

"The kids are going to live with us, you know. Are you okay with that?"
Less than six months after we meet, Ken and his wife separate, and he and I begin planning a life together. I develop a soft spot for his youngest child, Kennie, immediately. At six years old, he is a sweet, shy, loving little boy, and when we're together, I like to pretend I'm his mommy. I teach him to hold my hand when we go shopping and that three squeezes mean "I love you." His ten-year-old sister, Chrystal, and I take to each other easily, her soft heart akin to my own. I clash with the oldest girl, twelve-year-old Elizabeth, almost at once. Rightfully, she resents me. She is not just dealing with her parents' separation; she is also being asked to accept that I, only six years her senior, am dating her dad. Her dislike, coupled with my visceral response to her rejection, leaves the two of us at odds much of the time.

"Yes, of course!" I reply to Ken's question.

It's not that I'm lying or telling him what I think he wants to hear, it's that I know the mother of these children will not be able to leave them behind. I know she will keep them with her and they will visit us occasionally. Oddly, it is inconceivable to me that a mother can give up being with her own children. But that's exactly what she does.

In June, when school is out for his kids, Ken and I both leave our jobs at the mine, and he rents a small three-story condominium in Kamloops, a city two hours north of Princeton, where we all move in together. Mom and

Dad are quietly distraught, and Dad's jaw grows tight when he's around Ken, but once the alcohol starts flowing, everyone steps into character, and we learn to pretend we're a family. Ken's dad, a rogue of a man, welcomes me into the family and is openly critical of Ken's wife to anyone who will listen. He seems to believe that Ken has done well to choose me. Ken's mom, while also critical of Ken's wife, cautions me about investing too much in this relationship. I close my ears to her advice.

"Why don't you come home?" Mom gently suggests the first few times I go home to visit or she and Dad come to visit us. Her question annoys me. I wish she would accept that I'm an adult and able to make my own decisions. Anyway, even if I wanted to leave Ken—and there are times I think it might be the right thing to do—I would never admit I made a mistake.

At first I enjoy my role as the mother figure in our home, preparing meals, cleaning house, and caring for the children. But it isn't long before I see myself becoming tied to a life I don't want. I envy my friends who are either away at university or working and out on their own having fun, but I don't know how I could manage to do either on my own. I have gone from living in my parents' home, under their rules, to being oppressed in Ken's home.

I learn quickly that despite his insistence that the kids remain with him, Ken is far from being a hands-on parent. He has enough saved that he doesn't have to find a job right away, and he's more than content to stay at home. The children and I are totally reliant on his provision, which seems to be dwindling as quickly as the last days of summer.

Those late summer days establish our pattern for many years to come.

In the cupboard under the kitchen sink, there is a three-liter bottle of vodka with a pump on top that we call a Texas Mickey. I'm not a heavy drinker, but I enjoy my share of vodka and Clamato juice that summer. Ken, on the other hand, seems to have a drink in his hand from the time he gets up in the morning until he goes to bed at night. Every day bears a striking resemblance to my childhood weekends. Ken is often intoxicated before lunchtime; he naps for a while, then gets up and continues to drink late into the night. His behavior is unpredictable from day to day, and I'm never sure if he'll be happy or angry about something.

Early in our relationship I tell Ken I want to have a baby, and after we move in together, I stop taking birth-control pills. He is clear from the beginning that, while he will agree to our having a baby together, I'm not to expect any help from him in caring for the child because he's already gone through the baby phase three times. Blissfully, I agree.

In 1978, shortly after my nineteenth birthday, I learn I am pregnant. I'm ecstatic. I begin sewing maternity clothes and soft toys and buy yards of soft flannel that I make into diapers. I pore over library books about pregnancy and babies and know on any given day how big my growing baby is estimated to be. I'm convinced my baby will be a girl and plan to name her Laurinda—a combination of Mom's name and my own.

———

"Are you married to an Oriental man?" the maternity nurse asks when she gently eases the dark-haired, olive-skinned baby girl into my arms. Ken's heritage is Ukrainian and English, and her comment makes me wonder about my own ancestry. Is it possible to have blonde hair and fair skin and still have an oriental heritage?

I laugh and respond negatively, not mentioning the fact that I am not married at all. In 1978 it's uncommon for unmarried women to have babies, and despite my joy at the birth of my daughter, I'm ashamed that we aren't married. But shame is nothing new for me, so I ignore it and convince myself that I'm building a storybook life with the man I love.

A few days later, the day we're supposed to take Laurinda home, I sit on a black Naugahyde bench next to the pay phone in the hospital corridor. Ken has just informed me that his van has been impounded; the night before, he had been stopped by the police, who tested his blood-alcohol level and found it was above the legal limit.

"I'll get a cab and be up there as soon as possible," he says to placate me. "The kids are looking forward to meeting their new sister."

I'm nervous about leaving the hospital. I've fed Laurinda, changed her, rocked her. I've learned how to bathe her and care for the stump of her umbilical cord, but I'm still anxious as I dress her in the little white crocheted sweater, bonnet, and booties that Mom bought for her going-home outfit. I'm beginning to think they don't know what they're doing sending this baby home with me.

I hear the sound of Ken's cowboy boots in the hospital corridor before I see him. His hair is unwashed and combed in the greaser way he styles it when he hasn't showered, and I can tell by his gait that he's still feeling the effect of the previous night's celebration. But I'm determined that nothing will spoil this day for me. I'm taking my brand-new baby girl home with me, and Ken and I are going to have a family together—a family in which I will fit.

A few months later, as I stand beside Laurinda's crib, patting her back and trying to soothe her to sleep, I begin to weep silently. Ken is in the living room watching *WKRP in Cincinnati,* the three older kids are in bed, and I've just returned from the Laundromat with baskets full of folded, clean clothes that need to be put away. True to his word, Ken doesn't help with diapering, bathing, or feeding, and when Laurinda cries at night, he nudges me, as if he's afraid her crying isn't loud enough to rouse me. Asking for help would be pointless.

How can I keep this up? I wonder. I am so tired.

I look down at my sleeping daughter and wish I could crawl inside the crib beside her or even curl up on the red shag carpet on the floor and sleep. I'm physically and emotionally exhausted. Yet despite my fatigue, I am delighted to be a mother and am fiercely protective of my baby girl.

When school is out, Ken's three kids leave to spend the summer with their mother, and I feel like any other young woman making a life with her nine-month-old first baby and her new husband—except Ken isn't my husband, and he's still legally married to someone else.

He works only sporadically, and finances soon become a problem. Unwittingly and unwillingly, we develop a self-sufficient lifestyle. We grow radishes, onions, beets, peas, beans, kohlrabi, and tomatoes in a large garden in our backyard, and when the electricity is turned off for nonpayment, we set up a propane cookstove outside and make large pots of vegetable stew—assorted vegetables boiled in water with barbecue sauce for flavor. At night, after Laurinda is asleep, Ken and I read library books or play Scrabble by candlelight. The silver lining is that less money means less alcohol; Ken is sober.

But one warm September evening six days shy of Laurinda's second birthday, Ken suggests we go for a drive. I'm pregnant again, huge, uncomfortable, and a few days past my due date. I would like nothing better than to stay home with my feet up, but time alone with Ken is a treat, so I agree to a short outing. Elizabeth and Chrystal are old enough that I feel comfortable leaving them in charge for a short time when Laurinda is asleep.

As we pull out of the driveway, Ken declares that he wants to stop for a quick visit with a coworker who is upset over a recent breakup. I agree, requesting that we don't stay long.

The coworker is on the way to unhappy intoxication when we arrive, and he immediately offers Ken a drink. My heart sinks; I know he won't be able to leave until the alcohol is gone. Hour after hour I sit on a hard kitchen chair as the drunken coworker weeps, Ken offers comfort, and the rye whiskey flows.

When we get home, I weep tears of frustration and rejection, realizing that the feelings of a coworker Ken barely knows—and the lure of free booze—is more important to him than my comfort.

The following night, shortly before midnight, I'm awakened by cramping. I phone Mom, who is going to look after Laurinda while I'm in hospital, and wake the girls before we leave for the hospital. The next afternoon I deliver a dark-haired, fair-skinned son. We name him Michael.

I am twenty-one, unmarried, the mother of two, the unofficial stepmother of three, and living with a heavy-drinking man who is married to someone else. I tell myself I'm happy, but the reality is that I'm in over my head, too embarrassed to admit I've made a mistake, and have no idea how to change my situation.

I am still plagued with stomach pains. The doctors still find nothing amiss.

The Click of a Switch

It's been a long day; we went to Prince George to visit Ken's mom for the weekend, and the eight-hour drive home in a van without air-conditioning in the middle of a heat wave has been tiring. Ken deals with the heat by drinking a few beers but still insists on driving. He has no regard for laws against drinking and driving, despite prior convictions. His own comfort and well-being is more important. "If I'm not happy, then nobody's happy" is his frequent mantra.

Laurinda and Michael amuse themselves during the drive with an assortment of books and toys I've purchased just for the journey. For them, it's a grand adventure.

By the time we pull into the driveway, it's late afternoon and we're all glad to be home. Ken climbs out of the van immediately, pulling out the house keys and mumbling something about needing to use the bathroom. Laurinda and Michael, anxious to get to their rooms and their toys, jump out through his open door and run toward the house behind him.

I climb down out of the old green van and realize the back of my shirt is soaking wet with sweat. The warm, dry air on the dampness provides a brief respite from the stifling heat. I stand and stretch for a moment, enjoying the fresh air. I glance over at the lawn chairs under the shade of the weeping willow and consider how nice it would be to grab a book and a glass of iced tea and spend some time there. But there are things to do first.

I gather the books and toys the kids have left in the van and put them in a bag. Toy bag over one shoulder and purse over the other, I walk toward the house, mentally planning the next few hours. First I'll get the kids settled in a bath, where they'll likely happily spend a half hour or so playing and cooling down. Then I'll unpack and think about preparing dinner. Maybe later, once everyone is bathed and fed, I'll be able to enjoy some weeping-willow time.

By the time I get into the house, Ken has already opened a beer and is sitting on the sofa with the TV on, looking through the newspapers that accumulated while we were away. Laurinda and Michael are upstairs, and I can hear them dragging out toys and planning their next imaginative adventure. The house is stuffy from being closed up all weekend and the swamp-cooler fan on its wheeled cart is turned on and pointed toward Ken on the sofa.

He looks up as I walk past. "Get back out to the car and bring the suitcases in."

Hot and irritated, I respond sharply, "No, I'm going to get the kids bathed first."

Before I have time to register what's happening, he is off the sofa and across the room. His fist slams into my face. My head snaps back from the force, and I hear the cartilage in my nose crunch.

"I told you to bring the stuff in," he yells.

Pushing me fiercely, he grabs my hair and begins to repeatedly bang my head against the wall. He's much stronger than me, and his inexplicable rage makes him even more so. I begin to cry, not so much from the violence, but from my feeling of powerlessness and shame.

"Lazy bitch," he mutters with one final, dismissive shove.

I believe the white noise of the swamp cooler has prevented Laurinda and Michael from hearing anything out of the ordinary. If they notice later that my face looks different or my mood seems subdued, they don't ask why. I will never speak to them about this episode, or any other like it, believing that I can shield them from the angry words, the physical abuse, the alcohol-induced insanity in our home. This isn't the first time he's been physically violent with me; it won't be the last.

Later, I stand at the bathroom counter and watch blood fall into the white porcelain sink. I look in the mirror. My eyes are red and puffy, and the top of my lip is swollen and slightly bruised. Drop after drop of blood falls from the tip of my nose. I stare into the eyes of the woman who looks back from the mirror and wonder who she is. Slowly, I look down again and watch the sink gradually turn red as my blood continues to drip.

On the morning after it happened the first time, I told him, "I don't think things can ever be the same again between us." He said I was over-reacting, and I allowed myself to believe him. By now I know I wasn't over-reacting, but I'm in too deep to do anything about it.

Something inside me shifts. Then, as if I've found an internal control that allows me to deliberately turn off my feelings, I disconnect. I can almost hear the click of a switch as I shut down.

Marriage

It's one week before Christmas 1982, but instead of Christmas decorations, our dining room is adorned with white crepe-paper streamers, and two white crepe-paper bells hang from the light fixture in the middle of the ceiling. I'm wearing an off-white dress with long, lacy sleeves I found at Woolco, Ken is wearing his one and only blue suit, Laurinda is in a Strawberry Shortcake dress, and Michael wears a little suit we borrowed from a friend.

Yesterday Mom and I cooked a turkey, and we've prepared platters of cold bird, buns, pickles, and salad. Mom has baked three fruitcakes in the same cake pans that held her own wedding cake, and I've frosted the cakes with white icing and set a small, egg-shaped ornament that holds a tiny bride and groom on the top layer. The dining-room table is pushed against the wall; we'll serve lunch on it later. A handful of friends are chatting on the chairs I've arranged around the perimeter of the room.

Ken's parents arrive late, and I'm irritated when I see they've brought a few bottles of wine. We're short of money lately, and Ken hasn't been able to afford to drink as much. His dad embraces me as he enters the house.

"So he's finally going to make an honest woman out of you, hey?" he jokes.

I don't find the comment amusing.

Like most young girls, I once dreamed of having a traditional church wedding. Ken has flat-out refused to be married by any representative of a church, and I don't feel I deserve a church wedding because I've been "living in sin" for five years with a man who, until recently, was legally married to someone else. I have two children. The idea of getting married in a church is almost laughable.

Ken's oldest daughter, Elizabeth, is now living with her mom. Chrystal and Kennie, now thirteen and eleven, wait impatiently for the ceremony to start; they have plans with friends later. There will be an altercation between Ken and Chrystal later in the evening, but for now a fragile peace reigns.

Our house is home to physical abuse, verbal abuse, alcohol abuse, and rebellious teenagers. I maintain a façade of normalcy when others are around. I cling tightly to my hopes and dreams for my children and for Ken's and my future, no matter what is actually happening.

We've been in couples counseling. I was encouraged to seek help by my friend Jeanie one morning when she noticed a mark on my face that I confessed was the result of a moment of violence the night before. I'd tried to get Ken to agree to counseling in the past, but he always insisted that any problems in the relationship were my fault and he wouldn't see anyone until I got help for my own issues. But this time, with my friend's support, I called and made an appointment without asking him. Something about the way I presented it as a last resort must have prompted him to agree.

In addition to the couples counseling, Ken sees an alcohol counselor who says he doesn't need to stop drinking completely, he just needs to get it under control. I don't think he knows what he's talking about, but Ken, predictably, likes his philosophy better than the total-abstinence approach of the more traditional Alcoholics Anonymous. On the advice of our counselor, Ken finally filed for the divorce that became final just weeks ago.

I stand in the hallway waiting for Dad to join me. He developed gangrene in both feet after his toes froze when he was shoveling snow ten years ago. He's frequently in the hospital here in Kamloops, where the doctors are trying to stop its relentless spread. He has endured countless surgeries, each one removing a little more of a foot or leg than the one before. Today, wearing a new prosthesis and using a cane, he will walk me into the dining room, where Ken and I will be married.

Once we're married, I think, I won't have to feel ashamed of our situation anymore. I will be a wife. I am happy today—at least I think I am. But even now, moments away from promising to be with Ken until "death do us part," I suspect this marriage won't last. In the past few weeks, I've even questioned whether I should go through with the wedding. I'm doing it for Laurinda and Michael. They deserve parents who are legally married. I'm doing it for Mom and Dad. Over the years, they have grudgingly accepted our living arrangement, but I notice Dad's tight-lipped demeanor when Ken drinks too much and acts inappropriately. Somehow it's easier for him to see the speck in Ken's eye than the log in his own. Indeed, they both have alcohol-soaked logs the size of California redwoods in their eyes.

With all the guests now present, my friend Jeanie starts playing the wedding march on the organ we bought at the urging of Ken's dad during a more prosperous time. Dad takes my arm and we walk, slowly and carefully, the short distance down the hallway into the dining room where Ken stands waiting. The justice of the peace, in a threadbare brown suit, stands under the crepe-paper bells hanging from the light fixture.

It's a simple ceremony. I cry, Mom cries, we take photographs, and then Mom and I serve lunch. I am finally a married woman.

At some point during the afternoon, someone makes a booze run. By the time the guests leave, Ken is feeling no pain and is ready for bed. After Laurinda and Michael are asleep, I make sure Mom is settled in her room upstairs and Dad on the sofa in the living room before heading off to bed where Ken is asleep. It's our wedding night, but there are no romantic advances, no pillow talk about our dreams for the future. With Ken snoring beside me, I lie awake, stare at the ceiling, and wonder if I've done the right thing.

Shifting Sand

*Events in the adult adoptee's life such as marriage, pregnancy/
the birth of a child, or the death of an adoptive parent
frequently trigger the surfacing of emotional conflict around
adoption. Since pain, despair, and rage around adoption have
been deeply repressed for decades, these emotions are largely
inaccessible and potentially whelming.*

—JOE SOLL, *ADOPTION HEALING*

Chosen Baby

*M*y adopted state is never far from my mind in those early years of motherhood. I become fairly open about disclosing that I'm adopted when Mom and Dad aren't around, but if anyone asks if I ever think about searching for my birth mother, I always respond negatively. Why would I want to do that when I already have a family? But in the recesses of my mind, I can't help but fantasize about what it would be like to come face-to-face with my birth mother. I picture her young, with blonde hair and features similar to mine, and I imagine she got pregnant with me when she was a teenager.

One night I have a dream that my birth mother's name is Barbara Searle. I'm convinced the dream is a message to me. I pull out the phone book to see if such a person is listed, and when I don't find the name, I take a trip to the library and look through every telephone directory I can find searching for it in vain.

Once, when I'm leafing through a women's magazine at the Laundromat, I come across an advertisement for the International Soundex Reunion Registry, a service where adoptees can register, and if their birth mother also registers, they will facilitate a reunion. But I know Mom and Dad wouldn't understand; they would likely be angry and hurt if I tried to find my birth mother.

One day while browsing in a bookstore, I come across a little book called *Adopted? A Canadian Guide for Adopted Adults In Search of Their Origins*. I devour the book, marking passages that speak to me with a blue high-lighter. "The search often begins with the death of the adoptive parents, the adopted person's marriage, or some other deeply personal and important life event." I learn that the province of Saskatchewan offers post-adoption services and that it's possible to obtain non-identifying information about one's birth mother.

I tuck all this information away in the back of my mind, certain I will need it someday.

On a summer afternoon seven months after the wedding, Michael, Laurinda, and I are sitting under the weeping willow in the front yard with a pile of books on the grass in front of us. We've just returned from our regular trip to the library. Ken's three children all live with their mother now, and I've grown accustomed to a mostly solitary routine with just the three of us during the day.

One of my eclectic book choices this week is about cats. I've gotten to know an assortment of cats since moving in with Ken and his children six years ago, most recently two Manxes we got for Laurinda and Michael: Stars for her and Stripes for him. As a child I never had cats because Mom disliked them, so I know little about their care and character. In this, as in everything, I turn to books to learn.

Cats, according to the book, are more connected to place than they are to people; I can't help but wonder if I'm not a bit feline myself in that respect. I have always longed to return to the Saskatchewan prairie; I am connected to it in a way I can't explain. It will always be the home of my heart. The wide-open prairie and the hot, dusty summer wind exist within me on a cellular level. The oppressively hot and dry Kamloops summers bring to mind times of riding in the back of Uncle Albert's pickup truck over dusty prairie roads on the way to the farm to pick fresh vegetables for supper. Winter storms evoke memories of the sharp pain of frozen toes stuffed into last year's boots and of sitting in a bathtub filled with tepid water waiting for my icy legs to thaw.

I put the cat book down and reach for a blue hardcover that had caught my eye in the library: *Lost & Found: The Adoption Experience* by Betty Jean Lifton. I'm captivated as soon as I start reading; Lifton seems to poke around inside my head in way no one has before. As I read the fourth chapter, "The Chosen Baby," I feel my world shift.

Lifton interviewed countless adoptees as she researched her book, and while the details may have differed slightly, many adoptees were told the same story about how their adoptive parents picked them specifically from a group of many other babies. They were *chosen*. Lifton wrote: "The word 'chosen' was meant to act magically on the child's psyche, dispelling all curiosity about the missing parts of the story." But it hadn't worked that way for the adoptees she interviewed, and it hadn't for me. I had always hated the word "chosen." I didn't want to be chosen; I wanted to be like everyone else.

I read and reread the versions of the chosen-baby story that interviewees told Lifton. I feel betrayed. My foundation seems shaky when I set the book aside. Logically I know, of course, that Mom and Dad had acted in what they believed to be my best interest at the time; they had listened to the so-called experts who believed it was better to try to erase all pieces of the adoptee's prior life. But I can't shake the discomfort I feel at the realization that the truth that I was brought up to believe is a lie.

First Loss

*I*ve just returned from walking Laurinda to kindergarten. The school is only a block away, but I'm not ready to let her go the short distance alone yet. I like our early-morning time together; as we walk, she chats about what she likes about school and the new friends she is meeting. It's a special mother-daughter start to the day, and the crisp September air helps shake the sleep from my mind and prepares me to face the day.

I haven't slept well since the beginning of summer, when I started having constant and intense pain deep in my upper arms. It keeps me awake at night; only if I sleep with my arms above my head can I find some measure of relief. During the day I uncharacteristically consume copious amounts of buffered aspirin in a futile attempt to relieve the pain. I paint my arms with Absorbine Jr liniment on Dad's advice; it provides temporary relief, but the pain always returns. My doctor can offer neither explanation nor relief.

Dad is in the hospital in Kamloops again to have another piece of his leg amputated. He calls us from the pay phone on his ward throughout the day just to chat. For years, whenever the phone rings in our house, there is a cry of "Let it ring twice!" That's the code Dad uses to signal us to call him back so he doesn't have to spend his own change to use the phone. Every night before he retires for the evening, he calls. I tell him about our day and share stories about the kids. When I say goodnight, his last words to me are, "I love you, princess."

Mom often stays with us for a few days at a time so she can visit him in the hospital; it's a treat for me to have this time with her, and we're fortunate that Kamloops is just two hours away from Princeton. Our relationship has always been relatively close, but since the birth of Laurinda and Michael, we relate on a new level. As a mother, I am blessed to see how much she loves my children and how they, in turn, adore their grandma. One day when the four of us are in Mom's car going shopping, I overhear Laurinda whisper to Michael in the back seat, "This grandma is mine, and the other grandma is yours."

I enter the kitchen, massaging my aching arms. Mom and Ken are enjoying a second cup of coffee. The September sun shines through the kitchen window. The sunshine and my homemade yellow-gingham café-style curtains make a cheery morning picture. I put the kettle on for tea, and I'm laughing at something Mom said when the phone rings.

I pick it up on the third ring.

"This is the Royal Inland Hospital calling. I'm looking for a Laura Brauer, who is married to Edward Brauer. Is she there?"

I smile over at Mom. Dad must have asked the nurse to call her with a request to bring something with her when she visits later that day.

"Yes, she is," I reply, still smiling.

If the caller had taken the time to ask what my relationship is to Ed and Laura Brauer, she might have phrased her next sentence differently. As it is, she speaks bluntly. "Well, what's happened is that he has expired. Do you want to tell her, or do you want me to?"

I am twenty-four years old and have never experienced the loss of someone close to me. Expired? For a moment, I don't understand. Then—suddenly—I do. I'm numb as I hold the phone out to Mom.

Her face ashen, shaken by my reaction, Mom stands up and takes the receiver from my hands. I shuffle into the living room and drop onto the sofa. I hear her cry out "Oh, no!" and my tears begin to flow as shock gives way to pain. A moment later, Mom joins me in the living room, where we embrace and cry together in disbelief.

"I need him," she sobs.

From somewhere within my initial raw grief and disbelief springs surprise. Mom has always seemed so strong, stoic, and self-sufficient. I've never considered she might need him. I know she loves him, but need is something entirely different; I've never imagined Mom as vulnerable, but in that moment I see her for the first time as a person apart from being my mother. I wonder, curiously, what it must be like to feel you need someone.

In times of sudden loss, a gift of numbness comes after the first flash of pain. Without it, it would be impossible to take care of the multitude of details that need to be tended to after a death. The real work of grief comes later, often unexpectedly, and can linger for months or years. In this merciful state of numbness, Ken, Mom, and I arrive at the hospital, where we are ushered into a small room on Dad's ward.

A doctor soon joins us and says, "Mr. Brauer was up and about in his wheelchair for a time before breakfast and seemed fine. Then he returned to his room. He was found there by a nurse a short while later. We worked on him and did everything we could, but we were unable to save him." He explains that a pulmonary embolism resulting from his recent surgery is the most likely cause of death.

We're still processing this information as a nurse escorts us to Dad's room, where the curtains are closed around his bed; she discreetly steps away as we enter the draped sanctuary.

Dad's body is on the bed, his mouth wide open as if calling out. While the face belongs to my dad, it's clear to me that his spirit is no longer in the body before us. As Mom steps toward the bed, I turn away into Ken's arms and I cry.

Over the next few days, the family comes together in Princeton. Lori comes with a girlfriend. Aunt Edie and Uncle Albert catch the first flight from Saskatchewan. Uncle Bill, conspicuous to me by his absence, stays home, saying he's uncomfortable with the idea of flying. Dad's youngest sister, Joyce, with whom he and Mom had recently reconnected after sixteen years of estrangement, is the only member of Dad's family to come. Her presence unsettles Mom, who whispers to me in the kitchen, "She looks just like him; every time I look at her, I see him."

There is a small service in the darkened sanctuary of the Princeton mortuary. Lori and I sit in the front row on either side of Mom, holding her hands. Dad's open casket is at the front of the room. While we wait for the service to start, the three of us rise together and walk over to take one more look at Dad. I am sure I see his chest rising and falling, but before I call anyone's attention to it, I realize grief is just playing tricks on me.

For weeks after Dad's death, I move through the days on autopilot. I have Laurinda and Michael to tend to, so I can't give in to my grief during the day, but at night I lay awake, wondering if Dad is in heaven with both of his legs healed and intact yet seeing visions of him in the darkness of my bedroom, sitting in his wheelchair. Dad was a rock in my life, and I was his princess. He loved me unconditionally, even when I did stupid things like getting involved with a married man. Who will love me that way now?

Second Loss

*I*t's many months before the numbness lifts from me and I can allow myself to feel any measure of happiness. I'm not sure what grief is supposed to be like; I'm not sure if I'm doing it correctly. I don't want to appear disrespectful. Most of the time, I'm not sure what I'm feeling, and it's easier to feel nothing.

Eighteen months after Dad's death, Ken is out of work again, and this time it's so long since he brought in a paycheck that we're relying on government assistance to get by. I am deeply ashamed of our situation. For months we haven't been able to afford insurance for our own car; we walk or take the bus when we need to go somewhere.

On a late afternoon in March, I am at my kitchen counter pouring pancake batter from a well-worn Tupperware measuring cup onto a hot Teflon griddle as my mind wanders. I haven't talked to Mom for a week; usually we talk almost daily. I've called her every day, but there's no answer. I don't understand why we haven't connected.

A couple of days ago I called Aunt Edie in Saskatchewan to see if she'd heard from her, and yesterday I called one of Mom's neighbors to see if she'd mentioned anything that might explain her absence. I'm grasping at straws; I know she wouldn't go anywhere without letting me know. This morning, after much prodding from Ken, I consented to his contacting the Royal Canadian Mounted Police to ask them to check her house. I know

Mom will be upset, but I'm starting to worry and don't know what else to do.

The last time I talked to her, she asked if I'd told the kids about our tentative plans to spend Easter break with her. I said I hadn't, just in case something comes up that makes us change our plans. I've learned that it's sometimes best not to make plans that might fall through.

Why didn't I just tell her we're coming? Why didn't I just make it happen somehow? I chide myself for not giving Mom the gift of anticipation. She loves being a grandma so much and treasures her time with Laurinda and Michael. Our own relationship has grown even closer since Dad passed away. She's only fifty-five and still grieving the loss of her husband. Why couldn't I have told her we were all looking forward to a visit?

The mellow sounds of *Mister Rogers' Neighborhood* drift in from the living room where Laurinda and Michael are watching TV. I wonder if they find his program to be as much of a sanctuary from the turmoil of our life as I do. Ken's excessive drinking, unpredictable moods, and our tenuous financial situation weigh heavily on me. The slow-moving, gentle program takes me out of my world and into a place where life is lived without drama. In the make-believe world of King Friday, Prince Tuesday, and Lady Elaine Fairchild, people are respectful and kind to one another. Mr. Rogers tells me he loves me just the way I am. Too bad he doesn't know who I am. Too bad *I* don't know who I am.

Mr. Rogers tells Laurinda and Michael that it's a beautiful day in his neighborhood, and I pour another pancake onto the griddle. But even Mr. Rogers can't keep the truth at bay any longer. Something is wrong. I know something has to be wrong. As the bubbles on the top of the pancakes begin to pop, the front door opens.

Ken's footsteps are heavy and quick as he strides through the living room and into the kitchen. He walks directly toward me, reaches for the cord of the griddle, and unplugs it. I'm confused until I see the RCMP officer behind him, and in that moment I know.

It must be one of the hardest things in the world to do, to tell someone that someone they love has died. What words are there, really? This officer doesn't have to say anything. I know, just from his presence, that Mom is gone. The core of my being seems to exit my body, and I struggle to think of how I should react.

I look at the officer and ask simply, "What happened?"

"I'm sorry," he says. "I don't have any details. The RCMP in Princeton called our detachment and asked us to deliver the news. You will have to call them to find out anything more."

"Thank you," I say as I put down the spatula and run from the kitchen to our bedroom.

I drop onto the bed and put my face down into the pillow to muffle my uncontrollable sobs.

"Oh no!" I wail. "Not my mom!"

———

Ken and I are lying in Mom and Dad's bed talking before sleep. Somehow I manage to block out the fact that Mom died of a pulmonary embolism on the blue carpet beside this bed. I ignore the faint odor in the room of something I can't name. The numbness of grief enables one to do things that would be incomprehensible without it.

Laurinda is asleep in the lavender bedroom where I slept as a girl, and Michael has taken Lori's room. We've borrowed a friend's car to get here. The day has gone by in a blur as we've tended to the business of death: signing papers, selecting a casket, choosing a date for the funeral. When it was all done, we walked into Mom's house and I found her green jacket draped over the back of a kitchen chair, as if she was just getting ready to go out. How can it be that she will never wear this jacket again, that we will never share a joke together, that she will never know Michael and Laurinda as adults?

Tomorrow Ken will pick up Aunt Edie and Uncle Albert from the airport. Once again, Uncle Bill has chosen not to come. Mom's death will become real as we prepare for her funeral. Tonight I fall back on stoicism and practicality. Lori and I will inherit Mom's assets, and I can't bear the thought that because my husband can't—or won't—support his family, we might soon be living on what my parents worked so hard to acquire. Those funds deserve to be treated with respect and saved for something special.

"We have to get off of welfare and we can't ever go on it again." I tell Ken.

"Yeah, I know," he responds. "Maybe you can borrow against your inheritance and we can get our bills paid off."

I say nothing in response. I will never let that happen, I tell myself. With Mom and Dad gone, and with them my need to please them, I can do things differently; I can make some changes. I couldn't leave my marriage while they were alive because I thought it would disappoint them, but now it's an option. If I can't convince Ken to stop drinking, I have an out. As Laurinda and Michael get older, they will need things. I want them to have every advantage. I want the best for them. I want them to grow up without the blanket of financial shame we live under now.

I wish Mom had had something in her life other than her family. Neither she nor Dad had hobbies or activities of their own once we moved to Princeton. They made few, if any, real friends, and once Dad had to stop working because of his gangrene, they were pretty much left with just each other. Mom had nothing of her own to fill her life with after Dad was gone. She was only fifty-five years old; she should have had many productive years ahead of her.

My life will be different, I assure myself. I will find personal purpose in addition to caring for my family, and maybe that purpose will help provide financially. I will change my life. I will turn things around for myself and Laurinda and Michael, whether Ken is on board or not. I fall asleep with the vow foremost in my mind; my resolve is my mother's final gift to me.

Search and Reunion

*The journey is the adoptee's heroic attempt to bring together
the split parts of the self. It is an authentic way of being born
again. It is an act of will; a new dimension of experience. It is
the quest for the intrinsic nature one was born with before it got
twisted out of shape by secrecy and disavowal. It is a way of
taking control of one's own destiny, of seizing power. It is a way
of finding oneself.*

—BETTY JEAN LIFTON, *JOURNEY OF THE ADOPTED SELF*

Non-Identifying Information

I stand in the kitchen mindlessly washing breakfast dishes, finding comfort in my daily chores after Laurinda and Michael leave for school and Ken has left for work. It's September, the month of new beginnings and the first September without my parents. I am still grieving, and the weight of responsibility is heavy on my shoulders. Once I thought I knew it all, but now I'm painfully aware that I know very little about what it will take to build the kind of life I envision for myself.

I'm in a daze much of the time. It's been six months since Mom's sudden death, and I'm still feeling detached from everything and everyone, still struggling to come to terms with the fact that she's gone. Every few days I dial her phone number, knowing she isn't there to answer, but calling anyway. I tell myself it's illogical but can't seem to stop myself from picking up the phone.

When Mom, Lori, and I stood in front of Dad's casket, I was certain I saw his chest rising and falling. When Aunt Edie and I stood in the same spot eighteen months later in front of Mom's casket, I was certain it wasn't her and that a cruel mistake had been made. Startled, I had looked sideways at my aunt, assuming she had reached the same conclusion, but the expression on her face told me that she hadn't, that she believed the body in front of us was her sister and my mom. Grief had attempted to play the same cruel trick on me twice.

"Now it's just you," an older neighbor lady commented on learning of Mom's passing, and her words and the offensive word "orphan" flutter around my mind. In the quiet hours of the night, while my family sleeps, I lie awake, staring into the darkness and fighting down panic. I feel disconnected, like I am without an anchor, an astronaut floating weightless in the blackness of space outside the safety of the spaceship.

I've been busy in the six months since Mom died. Over the summer Ken, the children, and I have spent most weekends in Princeton so I can clear out our family home and make decisions about what to keep and what to dispose of. The activity prevents me from thinking too much, and that allows me to do what I need to do every day. I sort through closets and cupboards, paperwork, the ephemera of two lifetimes. I want to keep everything; every object is part of me in some way, from glass ashtrays with the names of places we went on vacations to Dad's old green recliner with the duct-tape patches on the arms. When I go through Dad's tidy drawer of records and documents, I hope I might come across my adoption papers but find nothing that even whispers of adoption.

I wear Mom's engagement ring and her diamond solitaire, and around my neck hangs the gold locket that was Dad's gift to her on their wedding day, the one she let me wear to feel like a big girl. The locket is a constant reminder of the love Mom and Dad had for each other and for Lori and me; it's a touchstone to the past and the family we were. Often throughout the day, I reach down and hold it in my hands.

The responsibility for settling Mom's estate falls to me as the oldest daughter. But Lori, not trusting me to treat her fairly, hired her own lawyer after an angry confrontation between us. Through the lawyer she sends a list of tangible things she wants from the house. I arranged to have them shipped to her and haven't heard from her since.

When we're in Princeton, Ken spends most of the time drinking at a friend's house, so day after day, weekend after weekend, I sort through my childhood alone, sometimes weeping and sometimes smiling as I lose myself in memories. Laurinda and Michael love being at Grandma's house even though their grandma isn't there; it's like a vacation for them. We bring their bicycles with us, and they play nearby amongst the yellow "dragon-snaps" that color the hills. In the evening they play with things from my childhood, like my old Spirograph.

On this September morning, back in my own house, I am mentally and physically fatigued. My body has betrayed me by developing what the doctor calls walking pneumonia, brought on, I suspect, by stress. There is no opportunity for me to take to my bed to recover, so I struggle through each day cooking meals, doing laundry, cleaning house, and doing my best to stuff down my grief so I can parent my children. The vow I made to myself after Mom died— to build a more secure and stable life for us— is never far from my mind.

I turn on the tap and swirl the water around the enamel sink with my dishcloth to rinse the soapsuds down the drain. Dishes done, I dry my hands on a threadbare waffle-weave towel, spreading it over the dishes drying in the rack. I decide to run out and check the mail before I start on the laundry. We're always anticipating receiving something in the mail—a check from Ken's annuity or, in leaner years, an unemployment insurance check that will help us make it through another week. I've become a master at juggling bills every month and deciding who will get paid and how much. Ken has a job as a delivery driver and has a regular income for the first time; it's not much, but it's more than we've ever had before and allows us to live, if not comfortably, at least not uncomfortably.

I pull the bundle of envelopes out of the large red mailbox on a post outside our front door and flip through them casually. I stop suddenly when I come to an official-looking envelope imprinted with an image of a golden wheat bale next to a return address that says "Saskatchewan Post-Adoption Division." My heart begins to pound.

A few months ago, I remembered the thin little book called *Adopted? A Canadian Guide for Adopted Adults In Search of Their Origins* that I'd bought and tucked away. It said that non-identifying information was available upon request, so I'd sent a letter to Saskatchewan Social Services to see what I could find out. With both Mom and Dad gone, and with them the possibility of hurting them by looking for my birth family, it seemed the right time to begin my quest to find out where I came from.

I rush into the house and put the stack of envelopes on the dining room table. With the letter from Saskatchewan in my hand, I sink down onto the couch and take a deep breath. I know that when I open this envelope, I am opening a door into my past, and once it's open, it will be open forever. I hold the envelope in my hands and wait for the beating of my heart to slow down; then I carefully tear it open.

Inside a tri-folded paper bundle is a picture of a baby wearing a white flannel nightgown that ties at the neck. I've seen the photograph before; Mom and Dad kept it, and another of Lori, tucked inside the pages of a telephone directory at the top of the hall closet. They kept those pictures separate from the rest of our baby pictures, and now I understand why: they were taken before we were adopted.

I imagine Mom and Dad receiving this picture in the mail as part of a sales brochure. "Today's Special—A Baby Girl!" The baby's eyes are big and wide, almost lost. I will be a good daughter, they seem to promise. Pick me!

I set the picture aside and unfold a yellowed and official-looking eleven-by-fourteen-inch paper with the Province of Saskatchewan seal at the top, followed by the words "Order of Adoption" in bold print. The document is dated when I was a year and a half old. I've seen pictures of myself as a five-month-old baby with Mom and Dad and calculate that I was with them for over a year before my adoption was final. They must have breathed a sigh of relief when they held this piece of paper in their hands for the first time.

Next I unfold a two-page letter, take a deep breath, and begin to read as though it is about someone other than me.

"Your natural mother was born in 1918 [and] had been married but separated from her husband for several years." I'm surprised to learn she was the same age as Dad. She was not the naïve young woman I've always pictured; she was more than forty when I was born.

"She was Protestant and of Dutch racial origin." So much for my childhood claim of German-Norwegian ethnicity.

"She was five feet two inches tall, 120 pounds, with a square-shaped face, blue eyes, medium-blonde hair, and a reddish clear complexion." The description, save for the height, could be of me. "Your maternal grandfather died in his mid-fifties as a result of coronary thrombosis. He was of German descent and had farmed all his life." At least that part of the German-and-Norwegian story was true. "He was five feet four inches tall with dark hair."

"Your maternal grandmother had deceased in her mid-forties. The cause of her death was attributed to menopause." I pause for a moment and wonder what that means; I'm almost certain women don't die from menopause. "She was five feet two inches tall with blue eyes and fair skin."

My birth mother had one brother and two sisters, and there was no history of major illness in the family. The information she provided about my birth father was that "he was born in 1913, married, and had been separated from his wife. He was five feet eleven inches tall, rather slim, with dark-brown hair and wore glasses." I'm stunned to realize that when I was born, she was in a relationship with a man who was married to someone else, just as I was when I gave birth to Laurinda.

"The record indicates your mother had two other children. She made private arrangements for one of these children, while the other remained in her care." Siblings! I'm delighted to learn I have siblings and curious to know what the "other arrangements" were.

The paragraph concludes by saying that "she loved you very much but was not in the position to provide the care and security for two children. She made the difficult decision that adoption was in your best interest." I wonder how many times the letter writer had written those same words. They sound like the stock ending to a letter of this nature and do little to provide comfort or closure.

I put the letter down, close my eyes, and lean back on the couch. I am surprised to realize that I feel very little. Isn't there supposed to be weeping? That's how adoption reunions happen on *The Phil Donahue Show*. I cry every time one of them is on—deep, gut-wrenching sobs overflowing with longing and grief as I imagine myself as the person on the program who is meeting her birth mother for the first time. But now that I finally have some information about my own birth mother in my hands, it's as if I'm floating somewhere above the room observing myself in the act of reading about her. I've spent so many years perfecting the art of stifling my emotions that now, when I want to feel something, I can't.

I unfold the final sheet of paper; it's an application for a reunion service. The Saskatchewan government will, upon an adoptee's request, seek out the birth mother to see if she is willing to have contact with the adoptee. Given the age of my birth mother, if I desire this service, it will be handled as expediently as possible.

There is no question that I will pursue reunion. Despite my discomfort about my birth mother's age, I'm intrigued by the news that I have older siblings. Maybe I have a sister to share secrets with after all. The prospect of meeting siblings is more attractive and less threatening than the thought of meeting my birth mother, but if I have to go through her to get to them, I'll do it. I'll try anything to find the family I belong to and to understand where I came from and who my people are.

For the next few weeks, I let the information about my birth family percolate. I get used to the idea that my birth mother wasn't a naïve young girl who accidentally got pregnant. My birth parents were both in their forties; why weren't they mature and stable enough to provide for me? What kind of people were they, anyway? The reality was apparently a long way from the *That Girl* car-accident story I imagined as a child. I'm confused about the reference to my birth father, too. The letter says he was married but separated from his wife. Was he married to someone else, as I first thought when I read the letter? Or was he married to, but separated from, my birth mother, in which case I would not be illegitimate?

All in all, it's not the story I would have chosen, but at long last at least I have a story. And now that I've asked for a reunion, maybe I'll finally get to hear all of it.

Carts and Buggies

One morning a few weeks later, just as I finish the breakfast dishes, the phone rings. As I hold the telephone receiver in the crook of my neck and dry my hands on a dishtowel, the caller introduces himself as Walter Andres. He's a social worker from the Saskatchewan Post-Adoption Division calling in response to my request for reunion services. This is the man who has the potential to lead me to my birth family. His name is forever etched in my mind.

"I have some news for you," he says.

Butterflies in my stomach are fluttering so much I fear that if I open my mouth one will fly right out. I sit down on the kitchen stool and answer with a barely audible "yes?"

"I've located your birth family. I'm sorry to tell you that your birth mother passed away suddenly a little over five years ago."

I realize I'm holding my breath, and upon learning I'll never meet the woman who gave me life, I begin to slowly exhale. It feels like there is a lump of putty lodged in the pit of my stomach, but I realize it's not the presence of something as much as it's a void, an emptiness, a hole that I now know will never be filled. I will have to learn to deal with that emptiness for the rest of my life.

I'm angry, and accusatory thoughts fill my head. She died on purpose to avoid meeting me; talk about the ultimate rejection. Well good! I never wanted to come face-to-face with her anyway. But the anger dissipates as quickly as it came, and I convince myself that I'm relieved I won't have to confront the emotion that meeting my birth mother would undoubtedly bring to the surface. It's my siblings I'm most interested in meeting. All I wanted from her, anyway, was my medical history and information about my heritage—at least that's what I tell myself.

Walter continues, "I've met with your birth mother's sister, though—your aunt. I visited her at her farm and she was very open to talking with me. She knew about you; she knew her sister gave up a baby girl."

It's a relief that my sudden and unexpected contact with the family won't elicit great surprise as it would have if my birth mother had kept her pregnancy a secret. At least she did that for me.

"They are a Mennonite family. Think of carts and buggies," Walter says in an attempt to clarify what a Mennonite is. "Your aunt is open to exchanging letters to get to know you," he continues. "While I was at her home she shared a few family photographs with me. She has many of them that I expect she will be able to share with you."

He has dealt with adoptees in the past; he must know that in lieu of an actual birth mother, a picture is what I want most of all.

Walter left my address with my aunt, and she has promised to send me a letter very soon. I want to ask more questions: What is my birth mother's name? Where did she live? How did she die? Instead I simply express my gratitude to Walter for putting me in contact with my birth family. It would be rude to probe further at this time.

After we end our call, I remain on the yellow kitchen stool, ruminating on what I've learned and trying to calm my racing mind. I am truly an orphan now. My birth mother is dead. But her sister is willing to have contact with me. That's almost just as good, isn't it? I come from a Mennonite family. Does that make me Mennonite? Why did she give me away? Who was my birth father? I have many more questions than answers, but at last I have a connection to someone who can provide the answers, someone who knows who I am.

To keep myself occupied while I wait impatiently for the promised letter from my aunt, I visit the local library and check out books on Mennonites. I pore over one with many black-and-white photographs of Mennonite women quilting and cooking together, searching the faces for features similar to my own. Are any of these women related to me?

I learn that the Mennonites took their name from a Dutch priest named Menno Simmons, who, in 1536, converted to the Anabaptist faith because he felt he needed to make a choice between the authority of Scripture and the authority of the Church. He believed that many of the traditions of the Church kept people from knowing the real Christ.

The European sixteenth-century Anabaptists were divided into three distinct groups: the Swiss Mennonites, the Hutterites, and the Dutch, Prussian, and Russian Mennonites. The Amish spring from the Swiss Mennonite group, and my people, the Mennonite Brethren, came from the Russian Mennonites who were forced out of Russia in the late nineteenth century. Many of them eventually made their way to Canada, where the first Canadian Mennonite Brethren church was formed in Winkler, Manitoba, in 1888.

Mennonites choose to live simply, but modern-day Mennonites don't separate themselves from the world the way the Amish do or drive carts and buggies, as Walter led me to believe. But his comment has shaped my perception, and as a result, my attachment to all things Amish is firmly entrenched, and my connection to the rich heritage of both the Amish and the Mennonites comforts and anchors me.

Though it seems like an eternity, it's only a few weeks after my conversation with Walter when a letter from my newly discovered Aunt Katy arrives. I hold it in my hand reverently as I settle back into the sofa. My first tangible contact with my birth family! I study the cursive script in which it is addressed, searching in vain for something I recognize, like Aunt Edie's familiar scrawl.

I carefully open the envelope and unfold the letter. The picture I was hoping for of my birth mother isn't there; I look in the envelope again, afraid I missed it, but there is nothing. So I read.

My birth mother's name was Mary Letkeman, not Barbara Searle as it was in my dream, and Katy describes her as "the kindest person I ever met." Kind to everyone except her daughter, I think bitterly as unexpected anger again surfaces. I can't marry the description of a kindhearted woman with someone who could give up her baby.

According to Katy, Mary was quiet and loved cats, but her letter contains little else about the woman who gave me life. What I had expected and hoped to learn is missing. There is nothing about my birth mother's character, what her life was like, or how it came about that she gave birth to three children but kept only one, and nothing about her relationship with my birth father. My thirst to know more is unsatisfied. I reread the letter a few times, still searching, trying to read between the lines for something that will make me feel connected to my aunt or my birth mother. It's as if I'm reading a letter from a stranger—which, in fact, I guess I am.

Later that same day, I pull out a piece of my best floral stationery and a matching envelope and reply to Katy's letter. I thank her for her willingness to have contact with me, tell her a bit about my life, and enclose pictures of myself, Laurinda, and Michael, which I hope will prompt her to reciprocate by sending me pictures of Mary. My tone is polite and almost apologetic as I reassure her I don't want to cause any disturbance.

Over the next few months, Katy and I exchange a few letters. I wait for each of hers eagerly, hoping it will tell me more information about Mary's character, the circumstances of my birth, my family background, and medical history. But letter after letter is filled with stories of Katy's life on the farm with only an occasional snippet about Mary.

Her most recent letter frustrates me almost to tears. "One of these days I will look through my pictures and find a picture to send to you," she says. "When I look at your picture I can see your mother in you."

I want to scream. Doesn't she realize how much I want to see a picture of my birth mother? Not "one of these days!" Today!

I'm treading lightly in this new relationship, afraid to risk rejection. I don't want to ask her for a picture of my birth mother, as I don't want to appear too eager or demanding. So I wait, frustrated, for her to take the initiative.

Face-to-Face

*D*espite Katy's seeming reluctance to provide me with photographs, time passes quickly during the months of our initial correspondence, and I don't have much time to dwell on my frustration. Eighteen months after Mom's passing and my vow to create a better life for myself and my children, I begin attending college full time. At twenty-seven, I'm one of the oldest in my classes, a "golden girl," as some of my younger classmates refer to me.

I love college; I love the sense of purpose and accomplishment I feel as I complete assignments and discover an innate knack for computer programming. I'm enrolled in a program that has a reputation for being one of the most difficult of its kind, and many of the students who are in class with me on the first day are gone before the end of the first semester. I'm determined to make it through and just as determined to make it in the allocated two years, although some of my classmates decide to cut back on the heavy course load and take the classes over a three-year period instead. Programming is my ticket to a career that will provide us with a stable and secure life. I refuse to allow myself to be deterred from my goal.

The focus of my life becomes very narrow. I attend Michael's soccer games with a textbook so I won't lose precious study time. I stay up late into the night finishing assignments and studying. The workload is nearly overwhelming, but my newfound sense of fulfillment and dedication to my goal keeps me going. I learn that I can get by on very little sleep and very little food, and my weight soon drops to under one hundred pounds. For the first time in years, the relentless pain in my body disappears.

My contact with Aunt Edie and Uncle Albert is reduced to short thank-you notes for birthday gifts, letters tucked inside Christmas cards with Laurinda's and Michael's class pictures, and a phone call on Christmas Day. I stop seeing the few friends I have in order to focus on my studies. In rare quiet moments, I feel guilty for sending Laurinda and Michael to an after-school babysitter, and I wonder what Mom and Dad would think about my choices.

"Your mom and dad would be proud of you," Ken's mom tells me.

Her comment almost brings me to tears. I hope they would be proud, but in the back of my mind, I feel guilty for not staying at home with Laurinda and Michael like Mom did for Lori and me. But I know that unless I do what I'm doing, our financial situation will never change, and my children will grow up in poverty. Every time I get another A+ on an assignment, my self-esteem increases, and gradually I begin to trust that my choice to go to college is the right one.

At the beginning of my second year, I purchase a personal computer—an IBM clone—with part of my student-loan money, so I can dial into the college computer from home to work on my assignments. Having Laurinda and Michael means it's impossible for me to spend long hours at the college like my fellow classmates.

After I get the computer, our friends and family complain constantly that they can't reach us because I have the phone line tied up for hours at a time. There is no such thing as cable Internet or digital subscriber lines; we have a long phone cord that I unplug from our yellow rotary phone in the kitchen, take into the dining room, and plug into the back of my computer. When I'm online, we don't have phone service, and I'm online a lot.

One autumn evening, about eighteen months after my initial contact with Aunt Katy, I'm at my usual place at the dining room table, logged on and debugging a computer program. It's one of the last warm evenings of the year, and Laurinda and Michael are out in the yard playing. Ken is having a beer and watching *Cheers* in the living room.

At seven o'clock, I log off, stand, and stretch to work out the stiffness in my back. It's time to call Laurinda and Michael in to get bathed and ready for bed. I unplug the phone cord from the back of my computer, plug it back into the telephone in the kitchen, and the phone trills.

"L-Linda, this is your Aunt Esther, your mother M-Mary's sister. My sister K-Katy told me about your letters," says a quiet voice with a slight stutter.

"Oh! Well, hello."

My heart starts to pound; I am speaking with a member of my birth family. Should I hear something familiar in her voice? Should it excite me like Aunt Edie's voice does? Does she hear my mother in my voice? So many thoughts and questions run through my mind in the space of the moment she pauses and allows me to reply.

"My husband and I are going to be going through K-Kamloops tomorrow. I was w-wondering if we could get together. I would l-love to meet you."

As it happens, I have only morning classes the following day, but I would have cut class if I needed to in order to see her. We make arrangements to meet at Riverside Park after my last class. My thoughts are in a whirlwind. I'm finally going to see the face of someone, other than my children, biologically related to me! Will she look like me? Will she like me?

After I hang up the phone I rush into the living room and tell Ken about the phone call. He knows how much this meeting means to me and seems curious to meet my aunt as well. I call Laurinda and Michael in for their baths and tell them we are all going to meet my aunt tomorrow. They know that I'm adopted and that I've been in touch with my Aunt Katy, but I don't think they really understand what any of it means.

After Laurinda and Michael are bathed and settled in bed with books, I go into busy mode, cleaning the house and boiling eggs to make sandwiches for lunch with my aunt the next day.

I am not about to allow myself to be vulnerable to the family that rejected me, so when I pull into the downtown parking lot at the appointed time the next afternoon, my breathing is shallow, but there are no tears threatening to fall.

It's just past noon, and the parking lot is nearly empty. I drive slowly toward the only truck and camper. A man and woman stand on the pavement beside it, and as I draw nearer I recognize the woman as my aunt immediately, even though I still haven't received any photos from Katy. She's what I would call slender, though not as thin as Aunt Edie. She's wearing a flowered blouse and dark blue pants; her hair is light brown and curled. More important, she has the same square jaw and prominent cheekbones I have. I am delighted to recognize physical features we have in common. I park a few spaces away from the camper, and when I step out of my car, she approaches me. As we get closer to one another, her face breaks into a smile and she begins to walk faster.

"L-Linda?"

"Yes," I reply. She embraces me gently. There is no outpouring of emotion from either of us—is stoicism a family trait?—though I glimpse a tear in the corner of her eye as we step back to look at each other. I feel a whisper of connection to her and trust her sincerity. Meeting her is almost better than meeting my birth mother, because my aunt's presence doesn't threaten or confuse me. I can relax into an unfamiliar but very pleasant sense of belonging.

"I have always known about you," she says. "I have prayed for you often."

I'm comforted by that. I feel loved and cared for by this gentle woman already. I wonder if Mary also prayed for me.

"You are part of our family," she assures me gently, resting her hands on my shoulders and looking into my eyes.

Esther and her husband, Karl, who has been discreetly standing in the background, follow me home in their truck, and later, as we munch on egg-salad sandwiches, we get to know one another.

"My s-sister had a knack for getting into trouble." Esther describes my birth mother as an insecure woman who was always looking for the love of a good man. Unfortunately her choices in men weren't the best, and she was taken advantage of more than once.

Esther adopted Mary's first child, a son she named Donald. Though he was raised by Esther, he knew that Mary was his birth mother—no chosen-baby story for him.

"Donald knows about you; I told him you contacted us, and he considers you to be his sister."

"I'm glad." My plastic smile and words are out of sync with the unexpected irritation I feel. Well, why wouldn't he? I *am* his sister.

Esther tells me Mary supported herself by working as a housekeeper for different bachelors or widowers, and a few years after Donald was born, she became pregnant a second time. This time she kept the baby, a son she named Merlin.

"They had a hard life," she tells me. "They had no m-money. Sometimes Merlin collected p-pop bottles so they could buy b-bread to eat." I'm thankful for the comfortable middle-class life Mom and Dad provided for me.

"When Merlin was a t-teenager he did not always t-treat his mother well. I think he felt g-guilty because of that later; he became very protective of her." Esther suggests that perhaps Merlin was ashamed of their lifestyle and that shame was at the root of his teenage rebellion.

"After Mary died, Merlin kept a trunk that had belonged to her. He has never let anyone see what is inside of the trunk—not even his wife, Sandy."

What could be in the trunk? I wonder. Something that reveals the secret of my birth? Is that why he doesn't want anyone to look inside?

Esther hasn't told Merlin about me; she seems to think he won't be able to cope with it. I want to meet my brothers, but Esther doesn't think the time is right.

"One day," she promises, and I wonder how she will know when it's the right time.

I ask her about the family medical history.

"Well, we don't seem to live to be old," she tells me. "Not many of us live past sixty." Well that's reassuring, I think wryly.

"I had scoliosis—curvature of the spine," I tell her. "The doctor said it's hereditary. Do you know of anyone else in the family who might have had a twisted back?"

"No, I don't think so," she responds. I'm disappointed. I'd hoped to learn that my odd abnormality connected me to my family, but perhaps it was passed down from my birth father.

"You are part of this family," Esther repeats as our visit ends, and she and Karl drive away.

I expected to feel different after meeting a bona fide blood relative. Meeting their birth family is the Holy Grail adoptees long for all their life, isn't it? Maybe I've watched too many TV reunions where there was weeping and laughter and lots of emotion and expected that to happen to me, too. But I never felt like weeping or breaking into giddy laughter during Esther's visit. Maybe being reserved is just my family's way. Maybe we have more in common than meets the eye.

I find it difficult to have compassion for the woman who had three children by three different fathers. It sounds like Mary was confused and insecure; I'm glad she gave me away, I tell myself. At least with Mom and Dad, I had a comfortable life and didn't have to collect pop bottles in order to eat. I'm glad she's not alive. I don't think I'd like her very much.

I'm happy to have met Esther and recognized physical traits we share. But I still have unanswered questions. I wanted to ask Esther if she knew who my birth father was, but I didn't want to pry; perhaps one day in the future, after we know one another better, I'll feel more comfortable.

Reunion

A few months later, we visit Esther and Karl at their home in Chilliwack, British Columbia. She serves us lunch and fusses over Laurinda and Michael, and I leave with a loaf of freshly baked bread, a ceramic bird she made at her ceramics class, and a container filled with lavender seeds—simple gifts any aunt might give to her niece. We speak often on the phone, and her gentle spirit and quiet nature continue to fill me with a sense of acceptance.

And then, about a year after the day we shared egg-salad sandwiches, Esther opens the door of her apartment, embraces me, and ushers Laurinda, Michael, Ken, and me inside. Until today, I've had no contact with either of my brothers. In fact, Esther has told Merlin about me only recently; she's warned me not to expect much from him. Today I'm to meet both my brothers at a restaurant, but I'm still confused by my aunt's fragile treatment of Merlin. He was four years old when I was born. Did he realize his mom had had a baby? Did he wonder what happened to her? Was he traumatized by the event? Or is his apparently fragile state of mind the result of something else?

We make small talk for a while, Esther fawning over Laurinda and Michael as a great-aunt normally would. Then she asks, "W-would you like to see some pictures of Mary?"

I can't answer fast enough. At last I am going to see the face of my birth mother. Ken, sensitive to what seeing the photographs means to me, suggests that he take Laurinda and Michael for a walk.

The first album Esther gives me is filled with three-inch-square black-and-white photographs held in place with black paper corners. It reminds me of the maroon album Mom kept when she was a young girl. Hers was filled with pictures of Aunt Edie, Uncle Albert, Grandma, and other people I never met but know about through stories Mom told. There was cousin Charlotte holding the cat that was almost as big as she was. There was the family at a picnic the day the tornado destroyed the farmhouse. That little baby? That's the one who was lifted by the tornado and carried to a field many miles away. He lived, but he had a steel plate put into his head as a result of the injury. Those were the family stories I heard growing up.

In this album I catch glimpses of facial features similar to my own, but I can't imagine feeling I'm part of this family's history the way that I feel part of the family in Mom's album. Nevertheless, I'm eager to meet my family, and so we carry on. As Esther turns the pages, she attaches names to the unfamiliar faces, and I peer closely at each one, hoping to see something that will connect me to them.

Then she detaches a photograph from its black corners and hands it to me. "This is Mary," she says.

I hold it gingerly by its white, jagged border. The woman in the picture is wearing a dark-colored dress. She sits primly, her hands folded and resting on her lap, her legs crossed at the ankles and tucked slightly back. Her hair is styled and curled; it's impossible to tell what color it is.

I lean forward and lift the photograph closer; I want to see her face. She wears glasses, the kind we used to call cat's eyes when we were kids, and the reflection from the lenses hides her eyes. I examine her facial features, noting the shape of her jaw and the prominence of her cheekbones. Unconsciously I reach up and touch my own face.

Breathe, I remind myself.

Esther turns the page and hands me a second photograph. In this one, Mary is sitting on a curb. Two young boys wearing dungarees and T-shirts sit beside her. They are all smiling. The boys are Donald and Merlin, the cousin-brothers. There are pictures of a vacation that Esther and Mary took with the two boys. In one, they are playing in a swimming pool and Mary is sitting on the edge of a chaise lounge watching them. She appears to be laughing at their antics.

You got to have both of them in your life, but did you ever think about me? I ask Mary silently, rudely, angrily. Did you ever think about the one you gave away?

I had expected more of the moment when I finally saw my birth mother's face. I don't feel like crying, as I thought I would; instead I'm hurt and angry.

I don't want you to be my mother; you're not my mother, I scream silently, like a rebellious teenager. The dichotomy between what I am feeling inside and my external polite acknowledgements of Esther's commentary ignites the burn of deception in the bottom of my stomach.

Finally Esther opens a contemporary, spiral-bound album with color photographs attached to sticky magnetic pages. She points out one of Mary wearing a flowery grandma dress, sitting next to a Christmas tree and holding an ornament she must have just received as a gift. A dark-haired young man stands behind her with his hand protectively on her shoulder. "That's Merlin," Esther says.

Ah, the elusive Merlin—he looks pretty normal to me. My big brother! I wonder what it would have been like to grow up with him. Would he have helped me with my homework? Was he one of the popular kids at school? Would he have let me tag along with him and his friends? Would he have been my protector? Would he have been upset when I played with his toys? Would we have had more in common than Lori and I did?

He's a good-looking, dark-haired young man wearing blue jeans and a button-down shirt. His hair is the same color as Laurinda's was when she was born, before it turned blonde like mine.

Esther points to a picture of a scraggy and bearded Donald next to a younger Esther and a woman she identifies as Donald's ex-wife.

I wonder if Merlin and Donald ever talked when they were young about having the same mother. How strange it would be to have a brother who was also a cousin.

In another album, Esther shows me a picture of Mary sitting on a sofa next to an older-looking man. She was living with him and working for him when she died. She was originally hired to be his housekeeper, but their relationship turned into a romantic one, and they lived together for a number of years. One day she was standing next to him near the kitchen table and simply collapsed—the victim of a pulmonary embolism, just like Mom and Dad.

In the color photographs I can see Mary's face a bit more clearly, but if she were still alive, I could meet her on the street and not recognize her. I see nothing familiar in her face; nothing draws me to her. In fact I am repelled by the face in the photograph. Is my anger protecting me?

When we finish looking through the albums, I clutch a handful of photographs, odd treasures in my hand. I feel both glad and guilty to have tangible evidence of my biological family. Am I betraying the family who raised me? I haven't told Aunt Edie, Uncle Bill, or Uncle Albert about meeting Esther. In fact I coached Laurinda and Michael not to mention her when we visited them. I'm afraid they would disapprove of my contact with my birth family.

Esther closes the albums. I put the photos in my purse, and we leave for the meeting with my brothers at a restaurant called The Pantry.

We enter the restaurant and find two young men and a woman sitting in the foyer. Esther greets them and turns toward me.

"Linda, this is Donald," she gestures toward the man standing closest to her.

"Hello," I smile hesitantly. He nods in my direction and returns my smile. He looks rough around the edges, and I can't see anything in his features that connects us; he looks like he has lived a harsher, perhaps more tormented life than his younger brother standing next to him.

"And this is Merlin and Sandy," Esther continues.

"Hi, Linda." Sandy smiles at me before I have a chance to say anything.

Merlin mutters a quiet greeting just as the waitress arrives to seat us.

I can't help but feel disappointed that I receive no hugs from my older brothers, no tears are shed, and there is no indication that they are either happy or unhappy to meet me.

Our motley group squeezes together in a booth: Ken, Laurinda, Michael, Esther, and Donald. I'm squeezed in between Ken and Laurinda and extra chairs are brought for Merlin and his wife, Sandy. Sandy fusses over Laurinda and Michael, and with everyone's attention diverted, I surreptitiously steal glances at my other brother. In dark-haired Merlin's face, I definitely see familiar features; he has the same high cheekbones and square jaw as Esther. He's good-looking and seems quietly confident. Is he masking the emotional frailty that both Esther and Katy have alluded to?

Sandy is blonde and bubbly, annoyingly so, and seems protective of Merlin, her hand resting possessively on his arm.

Donald is the quieter of the two brothers and lets Merlin take the conversational lead. Merlin, who has worked for a car dealership for many years, seems more interested in talking with Ken about cars than with me.

Perhaps they're as nervous as I am, I think, and they will warm up to me once we begin talking. But aside from Sandy's garrulous exuberance and the discussion between Merlin and Ken, the conversation seems stilted and forced. We could be any group of strangers meeting for the first time; there's no mention at all of our sibling relationship.

I want to ask Merlin what Mary was like and what his life was like growing up, but since he chooses not to ask any questions about how I grew up, whether I had a good home, or what kind of person I turned out to be, it seems inappropriate for me to probe. Instead I feign interest in the vehicle conversation and steal glances at my brothers' faces, trying to drink in their features and longing for deeper conversation.

After lunch we stand outside and say awkward good-byes. There is no mention of future visits. I rest my hands on Laurinda's and Michael's shoulders as we walk back toward our car. My children are my touchstones and my anchors. I was hoping to meet brothers who would want to be part of my life, but I'm not sure I will ever see either of them again. I open the door of our car, and before I climb inside, I turn toward them.

Merlin strides ahead of the group. Sandy and Esther lag behind, talking. Donald walks beside them and, just before I turn back to my family, turns toward me. Our eyes meet, and we share a smile before I get in the car.

Faith

So far, the reconnection with my birth family has been disappointing: first, to find that Mary had died, then the unsatisfactory correspondence with Katy, and finally the aloofness of my brothers. The only bright spot in the whole experience is Esther. I'm still glad I reached out to them; at least I have an idea of where I came from and who my ancestors are. I'm also comforted to learn that my own quiet stoicism seems to be a family trait. That somehow justifies it and makes it okay. Perhaps I'm not so odd after all.

And there is a whole new set of changes in my life, having nothing to do with either my birth or adoptive families.

The two-year struggle to balance family responsibilities with countless college assignments has been worth it; I graduated with a 3.87 GPA and landed my dream job. A few months prior to the brother-sister reunion, I started my career as a computer programmer at one of the largest corporations in the city. It's a well-respected company and a good corporate citizen, and that adds to my sense of satisfaction and pride.

My desk is positioned in a way that allows me to look out over the rest of the department. I love the view from my desk; it's exactly the kind of place I imagined myself working in when I was in college. I feel capable, intelligent, and on the way to the life I've always wanted. Every morning when I get dressed in a skirt and blouse, pull on pantyhose, and squeeze my feet into high-heeled shoes purchased from the discount store, I am thankful.

Our offices—cubicles, really—are separated by partitions covered in orange fabric. Atop my desk, next to my in-basket, a vase with plastic roses, and a picture of Laurinda and Michael, is something called a dumb terminal. The dumb terminal is somehow linked to another terminal—a smart terminal, I suppose—that sits in the center of the department. We have the dumb terminals on our desks to write computer programs. When we need to execute a command on the big mainframe computer stored in the back room, we go to the smart terminal to type it in. The smart terminal is the hub of the department.

Sometimes Wanda, the only other woman in my department, brings a box of Tim Hortons donuts to share with everyone and puts it on top of the smart terminal. Wanda is welcoming and friendly toward me and always patient and generous about helping me when I have questions. She dresses beautifully and seems to have an infinite variety of shoes and earrings that match every outfit she wears. Everyone, including me, seems to like her. She's a few years older than me, and the more I get to know her, the more she reminds me of Mom. She grew up on a farm in Saskatchewan, and we share a love for the prairie province.

Of the men in the department, Pete, the systems programmer, stands out to me the most. He is charismatic and exudes strength and integrity. The three of us—Wanda, Pete, and I—take our half-hour lunch break together every day. And like clockwork, at 10:00 a.m. and 3:00 p.m. each day, one of us stands up and gets the attention of the other two, and together, our coffee cups in hand, we wander down to the lunchroom for fifteen minutes of jocularity.

There is something different about these two; at first I can't put my finger on what it is. There is something that just seems *right* about them. They radiate a quiet peace and hope that contrast sharply with what is inside me. When I learn they share a strong faith in God, I surmise that must be what sets them apart. I want to find out more about their faith; I want some of that peace and hope for myself.

Consistent with the way I always approach new ideas, I go to the library, and over the next few months, I check out all the books on faith and Christianity I can find. I devour them, looking for something that will give me the same sense of peace and rightness I sense in Wanda and Pete.

It's the night before Valentine's Day. Ken is puttering around out in the garage. Laurinda and Michael are in bed, and I'm propped up in our water-bed, reading. When I bought valentines cards for Laurinda and Michael to take to school a few days earlier, I also bought a package for myself. Before I climbed into bed, I tucked them in various hidden places for my husband to find in the morning. I tucked one in his sock drawer, another in the coffee canister, the silverware drawer, in his favorite coffee cup, and other out-of-the way places.

When I hear the kitchen door that leads in from the garage open, my heart sinks. I can tell by the way he stumbles into the kitchen and by his incoherent muttering that he's been drinking more than I thought. His mood is foul lately, and his anger is usually directed at me. Either the dinner I cook isn't good enough and he sends his plate flying onto the floor, or he finds fault with the way I clean the house that reinforces his opinion that I'm lazy and selfish.

I decide the best thing to do is feign sleep, so I turn off the light and turn toward the wall, hoping he'll just get into bed and go to sleep. I'm wrong. He comes into the bedroom angry at me about something, and as he gets ready for bed, he begins his tirade.

"Stupid, selfish bitch."

He doesn't yell; instead he mumbles the words matter-of-factly, almost dismissively, but no less hatefully. I can't comprehend why he is so angry— I never can at times like this. I will not write most of the words he hurls at me; they are filthy obscenities he spits toward me like venom.

I put up an impenetrable shield and imagine the words deflecting away from me

Later, when he is passed out and snoring beside me, I rise from the bed and gather all the hidden valentines and throw them in the trash. Then I take the larger card I planned to give him in the morning and sign it with every filthy, poisonous name he called me.

When I wake up the next morning, he's in the kitchen having coffee and rolling cigarettes. Wordlessly, I hand him the card and turn to get myself a cup of coffee, watching him open the envelope out of the corner of my eye. He reads the card, replaces it in the envelope, and returns to rolling cigarettes.

What had I expected—an apology? Did I expect that being reminded of what he said to me the night before would suddenly make him realize he had to stop drinking? I'm not sure what I expected. I once thought that I could change him, that there was something I could do to make him want to stop drinking and I just needed to find out what it was. I'm starting to lose faith that will ever happen.

—————◆—————

A few weeks later I'm again in bed, reading one of the library books on faith. Ken is sleeping beside me. It dawns on me that the reason it's called faith is because it's about trusting something you cannot see or physically touch, and I won't find the answers I'm looking for in library books. I think about my God-fearing Mennonite ancestors and remember Aunt Esther telling me she had prayed for me throughout the years. Perhaps even Mary had prayed for me. Did their prayers for me include my coming to faith in God?

I remember my Sunday school classes at the Minto United Church across the street from our house on Seventh Avenue. I see myself in my white choir gown, lining up with the rest of the children's choir before service. I hear the adult choir enter the sanctuary singing "Holy, Holy, Holy" as we, the children's choir, follow behind them. I think about Pete and Wanda and the peace they have about them, the transparency.

I consider what I've read about Jesus: that he was righteous, spotless, sinless, and pure and that he provides a way for me to stand that way before God the Father. I think about the Holy Spirit, a counselor, the books say, who comforts and teaches the right way. And I wonder if I'm worthy of any of these things.

I've made bad choices. I knew they were wrong when I made them, but I made them anyway. My own choices heaped more shame on top of the deep-rooted shame that has always been part of me. I want to be rid of the shame. I want to start over. I want to be clean and live a life without secrets. I want to move into the light and truth that I sense around Pete and Wanda.

I crawl out of bed and pad down the hall to the dark, quiet living room, where moonlight pours through a small opening in the drapes and shines onto the tan carpet. I kneel in that light and in faith, begin to pray. I pour out my heart to God, not knowing if he hears me, but—for once—just trusting.

Surprise

A few months later, I receive a phone call out of the blue from the Saskatchewan Post-Adoption Division.

"I'm calling to tell you that you have a half sister who is looking for you," the caller, who identifies herself as social worker Bernice Donnelly, tells me.

"A sister! How can that be? There was nothing about a sister in the information I received."

"She's five years younger than you. There was nothing about her in your file, but there was information about you in her file. We were able to use the information Walter Andres obtained after you contacted us to tell her that her birth mother had passed away."

I am speechless.

"She's delighted to learn she has a sister and wants to know if you are open to having contact with her."

"Yes, of course I am!" I exclaim. "What is her name?"

"Her name is Wendy."

It was Christmas 1960, and I was one month away from my second birthday when Mom and Dad gave me a doll that, at thirty inches tall, was almost as tall as me. Her name was Wendy Ann. She had blonde curly hair and eyes that closed as if she were asleep when she was put down on her back. She wore a short pink dress with a black bow on the collar and matching panties. They took a picture of me sitting with that doll in a burgundy chair in our front room on Christmas morning. I'm looking up at her as if to ask, "Why won't you talk to me?" Until Mom and Dad adopted Lori almost a year later, Wendy Ann was like my little sister.

Now I have a real sister named Wendy. It seems hard to believe.

Bernice tells he she can't give me any more information until I sign a release form that she will put in the mail to me that day, along with a letter to me from Wendy.

"Once I receive the signed form back, I will telephone you and give you her full name, address, and phone number. Wendy is very anxious to speak to you and meet you in person."

We have our first telephone conversation a few weeks later, and I immediately feel a connection to her that both thrills and surprises me. My impatient sister decides to bring her family from their home on Vancouver Island to stay with us on the Labor Day weekend, just a few weeks away. As the date draws closer, I ask myself the same question over and over: what if she doesn't like me?

———

We pull into the parking lot where we are to meet Wendy, her husband, and children, and my heart throbs faster as we get closer to the red Jimmy she described on the phone. Ken pulls up alongside it, and as I step out of our car, a beautiful young blonde woman comes from around the side of the Jimmy, holding a potted African violet.

"Linda?" she asks.

"Hi, Wendy," I laugh nervously.

She hands me the plant. "I thought I should bring something but didn't know what to get."

She laughs at herself, and I kick myself for not thinking of bringing something for her.

I introduce Ken, and she introduces her husband, Paul. She makes a fuss over Laurinda and Michael, as I do over her beautiful blonde sons, Nicholas and Matthew. All the while, we are looking at one another, drinking in the similarities. Wendy is shorter than me and a bit plumper. She has the same cheekbones I recognized in Esther. She wears her blonde hair piled casually on top of her head. Her smile is bright, her eyes clear and wide. My sister! This beautiful young woman is my sister.

Everyone sleeps well that first night except Wendy and me. Fueled by endless cups of tea, we sit across from one another in my living room, talking, laughing, and getting to know one another.

"I can't stop looking at you!" says Wendy.

"Me either. I think we look alike."

We are both delighted by our physical resemblance, but it's the similarities in our personalities, interests, likes, and dislikes that I find more striking. Like me, she is family-oriented. We each confess to a tendency toward shyness, though there seems to be no shyness between us. We both enjoy reading and sewing, and we share a faith in God.

Most astonishing of all, Wendy and I lived just a few blocks apart in Moose Jaw until my family moved to Princeton. We attended King George Elementary school at the same time. Given the difference in our ages, it's unlikely we ever played together, but we might have stood next to one another during a school assembly singing "God Save the Queen," and I might have helped her cross the street safely during my tenure as a safety-patrol crossing guard.

We talk about what we each remember about Moose Jaw. At one point we both exclaim, "The Robin Hood!" as we recall the larger-than-life bow and arrow that followed us as we traveled from the North Hill to the South Hill.

I tell her what I've learned about our birth mother and about Esther and our two half brothers, as well as the mysterious trunk that Merlin refuses to let anyone open.

"Maybe she's in there," Wendy jokes, and we laugh irreverently, our laughter perhaps a defense against any grief for the loss of the woman who gave us life and then gave us away. I love Wendy's spunkiness.

We become sisters and friends that night. We're surprised when the first light of morning peeks through the curtains. We've talked all night, trying to make up for a lifetime of missing each other. I've never had so much to say to a person I just met.

Over the course of the weekend, I feel for the first time that I'm part of a family I fit with. Wendy gives me a different view of the world as she tells me about her enjoyment of TV shows like *Twin Peaks* and the impact that a new movie called *Schindler's List* has had on her. Her reality is as a stay-at-home mom with preschoolers who is working hard to start a children's clothing business; the chaos of my life is somehow calmed by the normalcy of hers.

———

I call Esther to let her know about Wendy. She is surprised; she'd only known about one baby girl Mary had given up. True to form, she immediately asks for Wendy's phone number and welcomes her, just as she welcomed me into the family a few years earlier.

Laurinda, Michael, and I take a road trip with Wendy to Chilliwack so I can introduce her to Esther. Esther and Sandy have conspired to give Wendy the opportunity to meet Merlin as well. Esther is firm in her conviction this time that Merlin needs to meet this new sister.

This sibling reunion also takes place in a restaurant. Sandy meets us there, and she is as bubbly and annoyingly effervescent as I remember as she positions herself in the booth so she can see the door.

"I'm going to meet Merlin at the door when he comes in and break the news about Wendy," she says conspiratorially.

Wendy and I exchange glances; I'm sure we will have lots to talk about later.

Suddenly, Sandy jumps up and walks toward the door, and when I turn around, Merlin is there.

"There is another sister," I overhear Sandy tell him dramatically. They speak together for a few minutes in hushed voices before joining us at the booth.

Merlin nods toward me in silent acknowledgment and reaches out to shake Wendy's hand; it's another bizarre brother-and-sister reunion.

As everyone settles back into the booth, I glance back and forth between Wendy and Merlin; they bear a striking resemblance to one another despite the fact that he has dark hair and she's blonde. I don't know if they share a father, but their facial features are more alike than any other pair of the four siblings.

Donald was twelve and Merlin ten when Wendy was born, and Bernice Donnelly told me that Mary took Wendy home for a while before surrendering her for adoption. He must remember her, I think as I look back and forth between Merlin and Wendy. He might have held her and rocked her. He might have shown off his new baby sister to his friends. Or maybe he was jealous of the attention Mary paid to the new baby and annoyed by her crying at night. I wonder what he was told when she wasn't there anymore. Was he cautioned never to speak of her again?

And then it dawns on me.

It is Wendy that Esther knew about and had prayed for during all these years, not me. She said she only knew about one daughter, and it has to be Wendy. No one knew about me save for Mary. I am the only one of Mary's four children who was kept a secret and rejected by her at birth. Involuntarily, like a familiar yet unwelcome friend, feelings of being forgotten, abandoned, and invisible bubble to the surface, but my countenance betrays nothing.

"L-Linda, will you ask the b-blessing on our food?" I hear Esther ask.

I don't think I can pray at this moment; it wouldn't be sincere. I'm the forgotten one, the invisible one. I doubt that God would hear my prayer anyway. I've been rejected and abandoned in some manner by everyone from the moment I was born. Why would God feel any differently about me?

"Why don't you do it, Esther," I respond.

Grief

I've been asked how I became open. I think there is only one reason why people change—because they are in pain, they hurt. They don't like the way they feel, the way they are experiencing life. I chose to struggle against that.

—BERNIE SIEGAL, MD, *HOW TO LIVE BETWEEN OFFICE VISITS*

Decisions

On hot and sultry summer nights I am often unable to sleep. Sometimes I rise from our king-size bed, slip out from between the blue satin sheets that are no longer cool to the touch, quietly slide open the patio door, and step outside, comfortable in my solitude and thankful for the quiet respite from my life. I sit on the step, hugging my knees and thinking about the future.

It's been almost a year since I met Wendy. We talk on the phone and write letters back and forth; we are connected, but I can't share my worries with a sister I've only known for a brief time. Despite our sisterhood, we grew up in different families and have had different life experiences; I doubt she would understand the craziness of my life should I find the strength to share it with her, anyway.

Since reuniting with my birth family, I've begun to experience a new-found strength, a glimmer of a sense of being on the earth for a purpose, of not deserving the name-calling and verbal abuse Ken heaps on me on a regular basis. When I learned about my Mennonite heritage and believed Esther had prayed for me throughout my life, my faith in God grew, and I felt cared for by both my birth family and God. Later, when I realized it was Wendy that Esther had prayed for and not me, my faith faltered, and I felt myself holding on to it tenaciously as an act of will. But I did hold on.

On this night I'm using the sleepless hours to clean my house. The repetitive back-and-forth motion of my arm as I scrub the kitchen floor is therapeutic. I should never have put the wax on it, I scold myself. It looked nice at first, but now it's going to be more work to strip off. That's just what I need—more work.

The mindless task allows me to let my mind wander.

I wonder what it feels like to lose control. I've heard of people "losing it," but I have no idea how one would go about doing it. My stoicism and need for control are so deeply ingrained that to allow myself to let go is inconceivable. Still, I find the idea strangely inviting.

It's hot in the kitchen on this mid-July evening, and we have no air conditioning. The window over the sink is open, but no breeze blows. The night air is quiet, and the temperature has dropped very little since the 95-degree afternoon high. The house is quiet at three in the morning, and the solitude soothes my soul.

Laurinda and Michael are sleeping, and Ken has already left. He drives a truck with a crane on it and works for a hotshot trucking company. He's on call twenty-four hours a day and often leaves home before dawn. I know he sometimes drinks when he's driving and that this puts his own life and the lives of innocent people at risk. Should I betray my husband and report him to the police? He would lose his driver's license and his job, and then what? My job doesn't yet provide enough to support our family.

Our life is spinning out of control. Weekends are crazy. Ken drinks to excess and turns into a different person. During the day he putters in the garage, where he has hidden bottles of rye and cases of beer. At mealtimes he slumps at the table and sometimes passes out before the meal is finished. The verbal abuse he routinely spews at me is getting worse. Something has to change. For years I've told myself I will hang on until the kids finish school, but I'm beginning to wonder if that's the best thing for them.

With the floor finished, I pull out the Pledge and an old diaper that I use for dusting and head to the living room. As I kneel in front of the coffee table, my mind continues its monologue. What if he's killed in a car accident? Who do I call first? What do I tell the kids?

I know a woman who got a knock on the door in the middle of the night to tell her that her husband had been killed. I imagine myself in that situation. It's not that I wish for it to happen, but I know it's a real possibility, given Ken's propensity for drinking and driving. I go to work many mornings not knowing where my husband is because he failed to arrive home at the expected time the night before. It's become almost normal to think that every time my phone rings it will be the police telling me my husband was killed in a car accident. Not only is it normal for me to do this, it's normal for me to act as if everything is fine while I do this. It's the same dichotomy I've always felt between truth and falsehood.

And yet it's not all bad. I love my husband and want our marriage to work. Over and over again, I plead with him to stop drinking; I try to help him understand how the drinking is hurting me, Laurinda, Michael, and even himself. I recognize vulnerability in him and know he's in pain of a different sort. I understand that his angry words and derision are directed as much toward himself as toward me.

———————

"I wondered if the kids could come for a visit."

My sister-in-law has no idea how difficult it is for me to pick up the phone to make this request, but I feel like I have no other options. Part of me wishes Mom and Dad were still alive to help me, but I also know that if they were, I wouldn't be asking for help to begin with; I would be acting as if everything is fine, as if Ken doesn't have a drinking problem, as if I am happy. There are Aunt Edie, Uncle Bill, and Uncle Albert, but I'm not ready to admit the truth to them either.

The kids are now fifteen and thirteen, and I want them to have a normal and fun summer vacation. I've started seeing behavior that concerns me. I'm uneasy about some of Laurinda's new friends; they're a party crowd. She has turned surly and angry; she disrespects me, she argues with Ken, and she's started smoking and drinking. Michael has gotten very quiet and stays home a lot. Though Ken's anger is usually directed at me, as the kids have gotten older and begun to express their own thoughts, he has lashed out in anger at them too. I feel guilty for the environment we live in, for the regular disagreements and the anger that permeate our home. It's all so different from the family I dreamed of creating when I was younger.

Ken and I are on the cusp of making a change. I've begged and pleaded in vain over the years for him to stop drinking, but it's becoming clear to me that it's not going to happen. I can't excuse his behavior any longer. It's time for us to make some decisions about our future.

"Why do you want them to come?" my sister-in-law asks.

I'm sure she is surprised to hear from me; we're not close, and this request must seem to come out of the blue. She has distanced herself from our little family over the years, and I feel her contempt for us. I'd like to know her better, but she has made it subtly clear that she considers herself a different sort than we are.

"Ken and I need to sort some things out," I tell her. "I just want the kids to have some time away while we do it."

His alcohol abuse is no secret to her.

"Have you tried to get him to go to counseling about the drinking?" she asks.

"We've gone to counseling more than once. It helps for a while, but then he goes back to the same old thing. I'm at the end of my rope."

"Well, how long would you want them to stay?"

All summer, I reply in my mind. Please take the kids all summer while I try to get our life back together.

Instead I ask tentatively, "A week or so?"

She agrees to a short visit.

———

When the kids are gone, Ken attends Alcoholics Anonymous meetings. We go for coffee together and talk afterward, and by the end of the week, I agree that we can try again. We make plans to go camping for the weekend before we pick up Laurinda and Michael. He promises vehemently that there will be no booze.

The camping trip is a compromise on my part; I'm not an outdoor girl, but I look forward to spending some time alone with my husband. We've talked a lot over the past week, and I've been clear that this is it; he needs to change if we are to stay together. I believe he's going to stick with AA this time.

We load up his van with camping supplies and head out in the direction of Prince George, British Columbia, where his sister lives. We detour into remote bush areas, looking for a place to make camp. Ken has brought gold-panning supplies and wants us to be close to the river. He has developed a touch of gold fever. He has staked claims in northern British Columbia, and he goes on annual treks with his dad, looking for the mother lode.

It's midafternoon when we arrive at a spot he declares to be perfect; it's really just a pull-off on a remote and secluded logging road. I'm afraid that if something happens, no one will be around to help us, but he convinces me we are safe. Besides, he brought his rifle along.

He parks the van, and we unload some chairs. Ken grabs a backpack that contains pans, jars, spoons, a small ax, and a shovel, and we set out through thick brush down the hill toward the creek. Huge black flies and mosquitoes buzz around my face; I fight the impulse to scream. It's hot, I'm sweaty, and the idea of swallowing one of the dime-size black flies doesn't sit well with me.

At the bottom of the hill, the creek flows cold and swift, and Ken settles down in one of the eddies and starts panning. I kneel down not too far away, use an old spoon to scoop out some of the richest-looking dirt into my pan, and begin the hypnotic swirling of the water that is meant to reveal the gold. It's a mindless task, and I find myself enjoying the moment, not because I anticipate finding any gold, but because of the quiet companionship with my husband.

This is nice, I think to myself. He likes doing things like this. Maybe if I get more involved with his interest in looking for gold, it will help him stay away from drinking.

We spend a pleasant hour panning, and he finds a few flakes of gold that he carefully puts in the jar he has brought. Then we make the same tortuous hike back up the hill through the dense brush and walls of black flies and mosquitoes.

While Ken builds a fire, I pour us glasses of iced tea and prepare wieners and buns for hot dogs. It's quiet. The heat of the afternoon gives way to cool evening air; the sky darkens and stars decorate the sky.

"Should we turn in?" he asks after we've eaten our hot dogs.

"Yes, I'm ready for sleep. It's been a good day."

"It has," he agrees. "It'll be good to see the kids tomorrow."

This is going to work out, I tell myself contentedly.

We crawl into the van. Ken adjusts the lantern so we can both read the books we've brought. Then he reaches into a compartment on his side and pulls out a bottle of rye.

The Grieving Year

We separate a few weeks later. I purchase a half-duplex a few blocks away from our family home, and Laurinda, Michael, and I move in. I feel like a failure; I failed to hold my marriage together and I failed to give Laurinda and Michael the kind of life I dream of for them. Within myself I know I did the right thing by leaving the marriage, but I grieve the loss of our family just as deeply as I would grieve the death of a loved one. Even though I learn in the Al-Anon meetings I've started attending that I am powerless to change Ken's behavior, the sense of personal failure and responsibility remains.

Sometimes I sit on the lawn swing in the summer afternoons, pouring my emotions into a new burgundy-fabric-covered journal. My foot touches the ground just enough to keep the swing in a gentle rocking motion, which slows as the words spill out in scrawled pencil lines that siphon the hurt and pain out of my heart and onto the page. The journal has become a savior of sorts, allowing me to express on paper what I can't say out loud to anyone. There is so much darkness in me that I can't trust anyone to share my whole burden. I write to get the pain out. I write to help myself understand. I write because it's all I can do.

<u>August17</u>
The pain is unbearable. I am overwhelmed. All I feel are waves of pain and deep, intense hurt. Where is it all coming from?

The ringing of the phone interrupts me. It's Ken; Stripes has shown up at the house again. Since Laurinda, Michael, and I moved into the duplex, the Manx cat has become a wanderer, often traveling the few blocks back to our house, where Ken still lives.

I feel a kinship to Stripes; we share the feline characteristic of attachment to place rather than people. I too want to wander the streets and eventually find my way to a place where I belong. I wonder if Stripes, like me, longs for our lost family life and for the house whose walls still contain and protect our memories. Every time I bring him back to the duplex, I wonder if he'll ever feel at home again. I wonder if *I'll* ever feel at home again.

I'm on a slippery slope toward depression and instability that draws me further into the vortex with each passing day. The self-help books I turn to say depression is a manifestation of anger turned inward, but I don't think I'm angry. Who am I angry with? Ken? I'm not angry with him; I'm deeply and profoundly sorry for the choices he's made, but I'm not angry.

Summer is unusually hot this year, and even if I weren't on the edge of madness, I would have trouble sleeping. Night after night I lay awake, lost in the middle of my queen-size bed, tossing and turning on blue satin sheets, searching for a cool spot and relief from the heavy, hot air.

Some nights I walk. The darkness helps me feel invisible as I walk up and down familiar streets, past houses where families live. Sometimes a house's lights are on, and I can see through the large picture window in front to the people inside. I find comfort in the sight of these families— they reassure me I haven't just imagined the concept of family. It hurts, and yet I vicariously experience a sense of family togetherness.

Once in a while I see *her*: a ghost of a girl with long, blonde, stringy hair—my younger self. Sometimes she is sitting under a street light with a book, and I can tell by the look of concentration on her face and the way she sits perfectly still that she is being transported by the book to another place, perhaps another time. I wish I could read a book and be transported to another world, but my mad mind can't stay quiet long enough to read.

Other times I see her in the distance; I usually hear her before I see her. She wears a plastic loop around her ankle, and attached to the loop is a long plastic rope with a bell-shaped object on the end. It's the toy Aunt Edie bought me many years ago. She jumps and skips, moving her feet so the bell on the end of the rope circles around her, and with her other foot, she lightly jumps over it when it comes by. She is nimble. Her long, slender legs know exactly what to do. Up and down the street she goes—skip, hop, skip, hop, skip, hop.

Most times she doesn't realize I am there, that I stand watching her skip. Other times, she looks in my direction and our eyes lock, and in that moment the fire in my belly is quenched and I feel whole. It only lasts for an instant before she breaks our gaze, turns around, and skips back up the street.

Sometimes I'm tempted to call out to her, to ask her to stop, but I hold back. What would I say to her? What do I have to offer her that would entice her to stay awhile longer? My desire for her to stay is selfish, motivated by my desperation to find peace of mind, wholeness, and relief from the torment that keeps me from sleep. I cannot care for my child self.

When I finally go home and fall into bed, the tears come. I can barely endure the emotional pain that envelops me. I plead with God to be merciful to and to take me home to heaven. I find kinship with the prophet Elijah, who "went a day's journey into the wilderness, and came and sat down under a broom tree. And he prayed that he might die, and said, 'It is enough! Now, Lord take my life, for I am no better than my fathers'" (1 Kings 19:4). After this prayer Elijah is tended to and cared for by angels. But I feel no comfort or care from angels or anyone else.

I stop attending my church. Our congregation is small, and I am the only woman in my situation; I can't bear to sit with happy families week after week. I feel I don't belong, and it hurts more to be there than to stay away.

Laurinda's rebelliousness worsens, and Michael falls in with a bad crowd. They skip school, and start drinking and sneaking out of the house at night. I can't cope with my own depression and their rebellion at the same time. One of the youth counselors I seek advice from tells me that at some point, parents only have as much authority as their teenage children allow them to have; mine allow me very little. Another counselor tells me that their rebellion and rejection mean that on some level, they have a deep trust for me that allows them to lash out, knowing that I'm not going anywhere and I'll continue to love them. She tells me jokingly to look at it as a compliment, but it's a compliment that threatens to destroy me.

One day, as I sit in the principal's office talking about Michael, I begin to weep uncontrollably. I want to beg this man to help me, but I don't. Instead I pull myself together and apologize for my display of emotion.

Another day, when I am talking to Laurinda's youth counselor, I can't stop weeping, and she recommends counseling for me.

———

John is balding and soft-spoken. Week after week I sit on a plastic chair in his office with a wadded tissue in my hand and tears falling down my face. I'm not sure what I expect from the counseling sessions. I long for him to give me some magic word to make everything okay, to make the constant pain go away. So far there hasn't been any magic.

"Why do you speak with your hands in front of your mouth?" he asks me at one of our first sessions.

I'm startled, unaware that the tips of both of my hands cover my lips as I tell him about the darkness in my heart. I drop my hands to my lap.

"I didn't realize I was doing that."

"People do that," he tells me, "when they are talking about things they don't think that they should be, when they are telling secrets, like they are subconsciously trying to hold the words in."

He's right. I feel like I'm betraying Ken, Mom and Dad, and everyone else who has ever been part of my life. I've never spoken openly about Mom and Dad's heavy drinking. I've never spoken the word "alcoholic" in the same sentence as the words "dad" or "husband." I've always pretended I'm happy, safe, and secure in my marriage. I've lied by omission to everyone I know about our home life. Worst of all, I've ignored the problems and allowed Laurinda and Michael to grow up believing that our way of life was normal. Every word that comes out of my mouth piles one more brick of shame on my head. Keeping secrets comes naturally to me; speaking openly and honestly feels strange, but I know if I don't do it, I won't survive.

September 10

I wish I knew where all this hurt is coming from. John said he would like to take me to that place, but I don't think I want to go there. Half the time I don't know what my thoughts, feelings, wants, and needs are, so how can I express them? I don't know where I end and others begin. I can't tell John how I feel because I don't know how I feel.

After our first few sessions, in which I cry for the entire time, John suggests I speak to my family doctor about depression.

"You are stuck," he tells me. "We won't be able to move forward until you get unstuck."

Reluctantly I make an appointment with the doctor I've seen since I was eighteen years old. I tell him about my marital separation and confess that I'm emotionally unable to cope with day-to-day life. It doesn't take much to convince him; he sees my emotional state, diagnoses clinical depression, and prescribes an antidepressant. In addition to my biweekly sessions with John, I now have biweekly appointments with my doctor and daily stress-management classes at the hospital.

Laurinda moves in with her dad. Despite their frequent personality clashes, he allows her the freedom she wants. My more conservative home, with its ground rules and expectations, is limiting and frustrating for her. Michael is becoming angry and closed off from me and is refusing to go to school. I'm at a loss as to how to deal with him and present him with a choice: stay in school and stop the recreational drug use or live with his dad. He chooses the latter.

My grief gives way to rage.

<u>November 29</u>
Anger is a feeling in my upper stomach. Anger is heat rising in my head. I am angry right now. I was wondering when I would feel anger instead of hurt and pain. I am so angry at God. Why don't I deserve to have a family? Why don't I deserve the support of a caring spouse? Why do I deserve the heartache my kids are putting me through? Anger is raging within me.

Breathe in…breathe out…and in between, don't surrender. These words become my mantra as I struggle to maintain control of myself and my life.

One day John hands me a pencil and a piece of paper. "Draw a picture of yourself in relationship with your birth family," he instructs me.

I think about Mary and the four children she bore: First Donald growing up near her because Esther adopted him; then Merlin, the son she raised; me, rejected from the moment I was born; and Wendy, whom she kept for a while before surrendering her.

On the left side of the paper I draw a stick figure to represent Mary, next to three smaller ones that represent my siblings. Then I draw a lone stick figure on the right side of the paper to represent me.

John looks at my drawing and nods slowly. "Now draw a picture of yourself in relationship with your adoptive family."

I think about Mom, Dad, and Lori. Lori, the one who acted out, always seemed more comfortable with Mom and Dad's overuse of alcohol than I was. She filled the classic "family clown" role in our family. I was angry and ashamed about the drinking; I always felt like a square peg trying to fit into a round hole.

I draw two large stick figures and a smaller one on the left side of the paper to represent Mom, Dad, and Lori. Again I draw a lone figure on the right side to represent me.

"Now draw a picture of yourself in relationship with your family with Ken."

I ponder the family unit I have recently lost or—more accurately—that I have recently dismantled. In this family, too, I seem to be the outsider. The irony that I left Ken to create a healthier environment for my children and that they are now living with their father doesn't escape me. I've failed them.

I draw a large stick figure and two smaller ones on the left side of the paper. As I again begin to draw the lone figure on the right, a lump forms in my throat and tears began to form as I realize that throughout my entire life, I have perceived myself to be alone, an outsider, isolated and insulated from everyone around me, rejected from the moment I was born.

March 7

I've been thinking a lot about adoption and the role it played in all the shame and guilt that has ruled my life. How can you ask a person to deny who they are and not expect them to feel deep down inside that there's something wrong with them? How did I come to know I was adopted and know at the same time that it was a deep, dark secret that I was not to talk about? How can you play mind games with someone by forcing them to deny who they are and expect them to stay healthy and whole?

Deny yourself. Hide yourself. It's not okay to be who you are. Act as if that person never existed. Act as if you're this person. How could I not be filled with shame and guilt? How could I grow up whole and healthy? The core me—the real me—died and was never to be spoken of again. I wonder what I would be like, had she been allowed to live. So many secrets. This must be the key.

March 24
And still, I don't know how I feel about anything.

April 28
The pain comes when my heart and my head aren't speaking the same language. John says I need to get to my belief system and work on changing what I believe. When my heart agrees with my head and my head agrees with my beliefs, I will find peace.

Homecoming

*I*t's true that knowledge is power. While the realization that I've always felt like an outsider grieves me, it also births the desire to understand why the pattern has followed me all my life. Week after week I work with John to tear down walls and unhealthy belief systems and replace them with the truth. My emotional pain manifests in the physical: my stomach hurts, my shoulders hurt, and at times my whole body hurts. With every step I take to get out of the depression, I seem to take two more backward.

Eventually I'm able to admit to myself that the grief I feel is real and only by acknowledging it will I be able to move past it. I realize I am grieving for the loss of all my families—my family of origin, my adoptive family, and the family I tried to build with Ken. The marital breakdown had triggered a deeper, unresolved grief for the initial rejection by my birth mother.

I can no longer deny that adoption impacted the person I've become. I can't ignore the shame unconsciously and accidentally put upon me by Mom and Dad. The so-called experts of the time counseled them to tell me the chosen-baby story as if it were my own. They convinced my parents that they could erase my past by ignoring it. It wasn't my parents' fault that taking this well-intentioned advice made me shut down emotionally.

I always knew somehow that it would upset them if I expressed curiosity about my family of origin, and the last thing I wanted to do was hurt them. Mom and Dad, for better or worse—and it was mostly for better—were my parents; I never wanted or needed another mother or father. How much healthier it would have been if I'd only been able to ask about the woman who gave birth to me, if I'd grown up knowing about my Mennonite heritage, if I'd been allowed to have a sense of where I fit in the world.

———

Grief work is hard, and I'm exhausted. I start making mistakes at work, which is the last place where I still feel competent. My manager suggests some time off, and when my doctor also advises me to take some time away from my job to work on my physical, mental, and emotional health, I find myself with four solitary weeks stretching out in front of me—four weeks in which I can write, pray, walk, and maybe begin to heal.

"Why don't you come for a visit?" Aunt Edie asks.

I'm reluctant at first. The prospect of driving alone across three provinces is daunting, but the more I think about it, the more sense it makes. Saskatchewan has always called me to return. Perhaps spending time around my family on the prairie will help me find my way out of despair.

I start the fifteen-hour drive in tears, and they keep flowing as the miles pass. I drive through the Rocky Mountains feeling empty inside except for the lump of despair in my stomach. I feel the closeness of the mountains as peak after snowy peak appears, but I find no beauty in the view; I'm too caught up in my own pain.

Then the landscape begins to change. The Rocky Mountains are in my rearview mirror and the horizon in front of me is lower, flatter. I breathe deeper as I drive farther into the prairie, the home of my heart. I've spent more years away from it than I did living there, but it's as much a part of me as it ever was. It is my motherland; it is in my DNA.

It's after midnight when I take the Main Street exit into Moose Jaw, praying I will find a hotel with a vacancy. It was foolish of me not to stop sooner; I'm so tired that if every place is full I will beg for just a broom closet in which to lay my head down. But as luck or providence would have it, I find a vacancy and sleep deeply under a white duvet in a queen-size bed. In the morning I rise to sunshine and find that I've reached the end of my crying time.

I take a tour of the familiar city streets: up Seventh Avenue past the house that Dad built, down Hall Street past King George Elementary School, and down Algoma, where Wendy and her family once lived. I drive down Main Street past the Uptown Café, where Mom and I used to stop for chicken-salad sandwiches, and past Joyner's Department Store, where the complex system of overhead cables that carried small cash boxes from clerks to the cashier at the back of the store fascinated me as a child. I drive past the majestic St. Andrew's church, where Mom and Dad were married and I once saw Prime Minister Trudeau descending the stone steps after the funeral of a dignitary whose name I didn't know. I stop at Crescent Park and walk along the paths where memories meet me at every turn—the library where I felt at home as a child, down by the river where Lori was once bitten by a cranky swan, the flowerbeds I had paid little attention to as a child but which somehow made their way into my unconscious memory all the same.

Refreshed by these memories, I get back in my car and continue down Fairford Street, past the Natatorium where we swam as kids. The tall tower diving board still stands guard. I remember afternoon electrical storms, during which we all had to get out of the water; I remember shivering with my towel around me, waiting for the storm to pass. I recall that Dad also swam at the Natatorium when he was a boy, and this prompts me to take a drive past the house he grew up in, 412 Moose Square.

When I've satisfied my need to immerse myself in the Moose Jaw of my childhood, I drive back up Main Street and turn right onto the Trans-Canada Highway heading southeast toward Stoughton.

As I turn onto the Highway 39 exit, I hear a ghost say from the back-seat, "This is the road I spilled my milk on."

Somewhere during the journey, my younger self has joined me.

When Highway 39 was new and the pavement was still black and smooth, I spilled a cup of milk, or so I was told. I don't remember. What I do remember, as clearly as the blue sky above me today, is that every time Dad turned onto this road, I remarked that it was the road I spilled my milk on.

"I have to go to the bathroom," the ghost in the back seat whines. When I ignore her she begins to kick my seat. "I have to go-o-o!"

I pull over to the side of the arrow-straight road, next to a field of waving wheat, stop the car, and get out. The hot wind whips my hair as I look out over the field toward an abandoned and broken-down gray wooden building, its roof sagging in the middle and its walls leaning precariously to the side. It looks like there's a slough close by, judging from the spray of cattails.

"Don't get too close!" I call as the ghost takes off running across the field. "It's not safe." She pays me no heed and continues to run toward the broken-down building and the dugout.

"I'm only going to wait a few minutes," I call. "You better hurry up!"

The silence settles within me as I wait, and I breathe deeply; I squat down and put both hands flat on the land, trying to draw strength from it.

On the other side of the road, in the distance, I discern the silhouette of a house that looks like one of the old Eaton houses. They hearken back to a different time, when you could order a house from the Eaton's catalog and have it delivered in pieces to your land. I've looked at real estate listings online lately; many of these proud houses are being restored to their original state and are in demand. On either side of the Eaton house is the obligatory row of trees that surround all Saskatchewan farms, planted to break the relentless prairie wind.

I see the ghost running toward me, her long blonde hair flying behind her like the tail of a kite. As she gets closer, I notice angry red mosquito bites on her brown legs. Those are going to be itchy later. She's carrying a big glass pickle jar filled with dirty water.

"Tadpoles!" she calls out. I know she'll want to keep them until they grow legs and morph into tiny frogs.

"You're not bringing them in the car!" I admonish her. "And watch out for the gopher holes when you're running. You could twist your ankle."

We get back in the car, and I pull out onto the road to continue our journey, the ghost silent now in the backseat. Further south, I begin to see oil wells bobbing up and down like donkey heads. I remember standing next to one when I was little and being afraid; they were so big when you got up close to them.

The unswerving prairie highway is familiar, as are the names of the tiny towns printed on the sides of the grain elevators I drive by: Drinkwater, Roleau, Wilcox, Milestone, Yellow Grass. I'm glad the elevators are still standing; many of these proud prairie soldiers have been destroyed in recent years. There are rusty combines and tractors here and there, abandoned on the field where they gave out one day, left there as a reminder of the past, just like the leaning wooden shacks.

The ghost lets me know she needs to stop again; I had momentarily forgotten her. I pull over and get out of the car to listen to the silence again but am surprised to find that it really isn't silent at all. I hear the click-click-click of grasshoppers flying and birds singing—meadowlarks. Dad taught us that they whistled a tune that said "I sang this song a year ago"; it still sounds like that. In the distance where the sky is now dark and angry, a fork of lightning reaches down to touch the prairie. Like me, it can't resist just a touch of the land. The booming thunder follows.

"The giants are bowling!" the ghost calls back to me as she runs across the field.

I smile at her exuberance.

Saskatchewan's warm wind wraps around me. "You are home," she whispers. I've heard that one can't go home again but don't want to believe it. I want to be home; I need to be home. The sky opens up and the rain starts. I look out in the direction where I saw the ghost running. Her face is turned toward the sky, and her arms are waving above her head; she's dancing in the rain. I can hear her laughter faintly in the distance.

The same rain the ghost is dancing in falls on me as I watch her carefree movements. I lift my own face toward the sky, and the cool rain mingles with the tears I am powerless to hold back. I close my eyes and let the rain wash the tears from my face as I breathe deeply, the scent of the summer rain like aromatherapy for my bruised and broken heart.

I should call the ghost back, I think. I should get going; Aunt Edie is expecting me. But I don't move; I stand still, let the raindrops mingle with my tears, and allow myself to let go, to weep deeply, to feel the anguish I've held in so tightly for too long, the grief to which I've been afraid to surrender. I grieve for the deaths of Mom and Dad, for the pain of not having them in my life, the sorrow I feel at having had them so briefly. I grieve for the death of my dreams, the breakdown of my marriage, the emptiness I feel inside, the mantle of responsibility so heavy on my shoulders. I grieve for my children, the mistakes I've made, and the mistakes I see them making. I grieve for the loss of my birth mother. And I grieve for myself.

When I am spent, I open my eyes. The rain is just a drizzle now, and in the distance there is a break in the clouds. I turn my head, prepared to call the ghost back, but I'm surprised to see her standing next to me. She is simply standing there, looking up at me with eyes as big as plates, her hair like long wet strings. I squat down and gently take her face in my hands.

"Thank you for coming with me today," I tell her.

She smiles, and we get back in the car; this time I invite the ghost to sit in the front, beside me. I pull out onto the prairie road and turn the car around in the opposite direction from the way we were traveling before.

"What are you doing?" the ghost asks. "Stoughton is that way."

"I know. It's not much farther, and we've got plenty of time."

"But where are we going?" she asks.

"We're going back to get your tadpoles."

Her face lights up with a big smile, and I reach over and take her hand in mine.

Evening Visit

"Hi, kiddo!"

Aunt Edie and Uncle Bill greet me with hugs and big smiles. Aunt Edie resembles Grandma more every time I see her, but she's as slender and nimble as ever—a young sixty-six. Uncle Bill looks like he's gained a bit of weight since I saw him last and walks with a cane. He's getting older.

Aunt Edie has planned a simple supper of pork chops, potatoes, peas, homemade buns, and dill pickles. I peel potatoes at the sink and look out over the familiar street, past the houses on the other side and toward the prairie beyond. I'm home. I feel embraced and loved. I wish I could stay here forever.

After the potatoes are peeled, Aunt Edie puts them on to boil and I head outside to visit with Uncle Bill while he barbecues the pork chops.

"Do you still have the ponies, Uncle Bill?" They bought Shetland ponies for Myra when she was a child, and they later became heavily involved in chariot racing.

"Oh, no, we got rid of them some time ago." He speaks with the same slow drawl I remember. "I can't ride in the chariots anymore, and Myra isn't interested in them."

I feel a twinge of jealousy at the mention of Myra. I wish I'd been able to spend as much time with Aunt Edie and Uncle Bill as she has. Of course, since she still lives in Stoughton and I live two provinces away, that's just the way things turned out.

"I bet you miss going to the races."

"Oh, we still go to the races. We just go to watch with our friends now."

We chat pleasantly about the ponies and how the crops are doing this year.

"We'll take a drive over to see Albert tomorrow," he suggests as we walk back toward the house when the pork chops are cooked.

"That would be great!" I can't wait to see my uncle again and spend time in the tiny house where Mom grew up.

After supper, Aunt Edie and I clean up and Uncle Bill goes to watch the evening news. When the dishes are put away and the long prairie evening stretches out in front of us, Aunt Edie and I drive the short distance to the house of Uncle Bill's sister Helen for a visit. I don't remember Helen from my childhood, but my aunt tells me she would love to see me after all this time, so I assume she must remember me.

We enter through the back door, the family entrance, and climb three stairs up into the kitchen. The windows are all open and a slight breeze blows, making the temperature inside comfortable; it's still well over 80 degrees outside. Helen greets us with tall glasses of sweet iced tea and motions for us to sit down at the large mahogany table that fills the eating area.

We have barely sat down when I see Helen's eyes widen as she looks at Aunt Edie, who is sitting next to me.

"Edith?" she exclaims.

Aunt Edie's lips are moving like a baby's blowing bubbles. Something is terribly wrong. Her gaze is blank and her body still but for the burbling of her lips expressing air. Helen and I leap to our feet. I race to the phone to call for an ambulance.

"Do you have 9-1-1?" I quickly ask.

"Oh, no," Helen tells me, her eyes wide. "Look in the phone book for the number of the ambulance."

I open up the thin phone book that covers several towns and search inside the front cover for the number. "Helen! How many numbers do I have to dial? Is it still four? Or do I have to dial all seven?"

She's confused, which makes me confused. I dial the four numbers, and the line keeps ringing. I dial seven, and the line is busy.

I remember that Myra works in a nursing home; she must know first aid. "Helen, do you know Myra's phone number?"

"It's written down right there," she says, pointing toward a piece of paper taped to the wall above the phone.

I manage to get in touch with Myra, and she says she'll be right over. Meanwhile, Helen has returned from the bathroom with a wet facecloth that she tells me to put on Aunt Edie's forehead—the cure-all for everything when I was a child. I know it isn't going to help but I do as Helen instructs. In just a few minutes, Myra races into the house, assesses the situation, and calls for the ambulance.

I pace and pray, horrified. I don't know CPR and don't even know if CPR would help, but I tell myself I should be doing something. All I can manage is to whisper "Jesus, Jesus," as I pace and my aunt continues to burble air. I sense that she's already gone, like Dad was already gone from his body the last time I saw him in the hospital, and that this is just her body going through the process of shutting down.

When the paramedics arrive they move her to the floor and attach a machine to her chest. "No heartbeat detected—check patient," the machine's voice says over and over again, confirming my suspicions.

Come Home

Uncle Bill and I sit at the kitchen table with the United Church minister the next day, planning Aunt Edie's funeral. In the corner behind the table is a small telephone chair. In my mind's eye I can see Aunt Edie sitting on its padded seat, her fingers dialing Uncle Albert's number to invite him to come for supper. I remember Mom and Dad scolding Lori and me for twirling on the swivel chairs where we now sit. I see the remaining pieces of Aunt Edie's American Beauty china. It's incomprehensible to me that just the day before I was talking to Aunt Edie and now she's gone.

The minister, a middle-aged woman with short brown hair, asks if I would like to read a piece of scripture at the funeral. Of course I want to honor my aunt in this manner. She hands me a piece of paper with an unfamiliar passage from the Apocrypha. I would rather read a passage from the Bible, but if this is what she wants me to read, so be it.

The day of the funeral seems to be the hottest day of the summer; the temperature inside the tiny wooden United Church is even higher than it is outside. Uncle Bill asks the minister to announce that it's okay for the men to remove their suit jackets.

Myra had taken me to Weyburn the previous day to buy something appropriate to wear. I sit in the front pew between Uncle Albert and Uncle Bill and reach my hands over on each side to rest on theirs in a gesture of comfort. Uncle Bill struggles to maintain composure and frequently reaches into his pocket to get a handkerchief to wipe his eyes. Uncle Albert is stoically looking straight ahead, though he smiles slightly at me when I rest my hand on his.

We contacted Lori. She couldn't come for the funeral but promised to come as soon as she can.

From behind us, in a loft above the congregation, the choir sings the hymn "Softly and Tenderly." Their voices blend in a heavenly chorus on the refrain "come home, come home." Their voices wrap around me, penetrating my being and drawing me in.

When the time comes for me to read, I stand and walk up the steps to the pulpit. Before I begin, I look out across the pews. I recognize very few of the people in the congregation, but I'm sure many of them recognize a younger version of me.

Later, at the local Royal Canadian Legion hall, the church ladies serve tea and a light lunch just as they have done for countless funerals in the past. Distant family members come to greet me and embrace me. Despite the sorrow of the day, it feels like a homecoming of sorts, and I allow myself to enjoy the love that seems to be offered freely.

———

Later, when everyone has left and Uncle Bill and I are alone at his house, he breaks down.

"Would you stay with me?" he asks through tear-filled eyes, and I see fear mixed with grief.

I embrace him and mumble inadequate words of comfort. More than once over the course of the evening he embraces me and asks me to stay with him; I know it's the grief talking. I consider what it would take for me to leave my job and move to Saskatchewan. As much as I feel the prairie is my home, I know it's not practical for me to stay.

A few days later, we are sitting in the living room one evening when he hands me a diamond-and-ruby ring and some other jewelry of Aunt Edie's.

"I bought her that ring last Christmas," he says, "to replace the one your mother had that went missing—the one that belonged to their mother."

When Grandma died, Mom got a ring that had a faux diamond in the center and two faux rubies on either side. One of the red stones was missing, and she had it replaced with one that never quite matched the other one. The ring wasn't worth anything monetarily, but it meant everything to my mom. It went missing one weekend when Ken and I and his three children were visiting. We were never able to determine exactly what happened to it or to another one that went missing that weekend, and no confessions were ever offered, though we tried to learn the truth.

When I try the ring on, Uncle Bill comments on the diamond solitaire I'm wearing on my right hand.

"It was Mom's," I tell him. It's the ring Dad promised to buy Mom when they married. I wear it always.

Somehow the conversation turns to my adoption, and Uncle Bill asks me a question I've never been asked by a member of my family before: "Do you ever think about your real mother?"

I hold my breath, and a million thoughts pass through my mind in the space of a few seconds. First of all, Mom is my real mother. Should I confess that I've reached out to my birth family? Should I tell him I know a good part of my heritage at last? Or should I keep up the façade? I decide to honor the truth; I've been on a quest for truth for too long to answer any other way.

"Actually, I've been able to contact my birth family, but my birth mother had already died."

Uncle Bill doesn't say much in response, and I'm not sure what he's thinking. I'm convinced, however, that telling the truth was the right thing to do.

A few days later, friends of Aunt Edie and Uncle Bill who were not able to come for the funeral arrive to spend some time with him. The couple and their four girls are welcomed into Uncle Bill's home and there is room enough for all seven guests to stay comfortably, even with me still there. But now that Uncle Bill's friends are there, I feel better about leaving him. I have to go home. It's time for me to go back to work and pick up the pieces of my life.

Family

*I was left to make sense of this family that
I was a part of and yet wasn't.*

—LINDA JOY MYERS, *DON'T CALL ME MOTHER*

Another Family

I'm deeply shaken by Aunt Edie's sudden death. I talk with Uncle Bill and Uncle Albert on the phone every so often; I know her death has left a huge void in their lives. Yet despite my own sorrow at losing my beloved aunt and my shock at being there when she died, my grief is different this time. It seems to propel me forward instead of sucking me back into the vortex of depression.

I return to my job and get involved with a new church. I see John a few more times and agree with him when he tells me he believes our work is finished. I have made it to the other side of my depression. My work with him was deep and painful, but necessary. I'm even thankful for that dark season that brought me wisdom and the realization that I was grieving much more than the loss of a marriage—I was grieving the loss of myself.

I've come to realize that separation from my family of origin impacted me in ways I didn't realize. For most of my life, I haven't had a sense of who I am; it wasn't always evident to me where I ended and other people began. I got used to feeling I didn't fit in, no matter where I was or who I was with. I became an expert at holding people at arm's length, not trusting anyone. Losing my first family, then my second family when Mom and Dad died, and my third when Ken and I separated and Laurinda and Michael went to live with him, left me feeling completely abandoned, and no matter how many times I told myself that none of the circumstances were my fault, I had an inherent sense that there was something wrong with me that prevented me from having what I so desperately wanted: a family.

I had been willing to go against what I knew to be right when I started the relationship with Ken, all for the sake of my self-esteem and the desire to create a family. Later, I overlooked unhealthy and destructive behavior in order to maintain the family he and I created. I did no justice to his children and caused harm to Laurinda and Michael. There are many things in my life I'm not proud of, but the work with John has helped me see it for what it is and forgive myself.

I'm content with my life; I'm active in my church and, after forcing myself to push through my inherent shyness to step out, have been rewarded with new friends coming into my life. I feel ready to move forward.

———

I've lived in Kamloops for over twenty years, and there are faces I recognize. Some are from the TV news or the newspaper. Others belong to people I've attended a class with or to the parents of Laurinda's and Michael's classmates, people I've seen when I helped out at school or attended ball games. Still others I recognize from my seat in the back row at church.

One Sunday after the service, a man with one of the familiar faces approaches me in the church foyer with an invitation. "Do you want to go for lunch?"

I recognize Gerry from places I can no longer recall. I know his son Brandon played on Michael's baseball team one season, and they took karate lessons at the same time one year. When I first saw Gerry at church, I recognized him, and since we attend the same Bible study, it's natural for me to feel comfortable talking to him. He isn't a stranger. So his casual lunch invitation neither fills me with dread nor makes me giddy with excitement. We're just two acquaintances sharing a lunch and some conversation.

I'm not interested in dating. I can't imagine allowing myself to get close to anyone that way again. Since my marriage ended, I've gone on one date—thanks to Wendy, who tried to play matchmaker by fixing me up with a man she knew in Kamloops. It was a disaster. I knew when he picked me up that I'd be counting the seconds until we finished dinner and I could return home. I politely declined his invitation to see a movie after dinner, and I left no opening for a future engagement. No more blind dates for me.

With Gerry, I'm comfortable from the beginning. He makes me laugh. He treats me the way I want to be treated; he's respectful, kind, thoughtful. We complement each other: he's a dreamer, and my feet are firmly nailed to the ground. The first lunch leads to another, which leads to another, and in time I begin to think about possibility and dreams I've given up on— dreams of family.

———

I don't want a fuss; I'm forty years old, and we've both been married before. I'd be happy with just the two of us standing before our pastor in his office, but Gerry insists on a church wedding. We choose the little church I first attended, the one I left because it was too painful to be alone among family units. Somehow it seems right to marry Gerry in that little church. I'm going to have my own family after all.

It's a beautiful day at the end of April, one year after that first lunch date, when we arrive at the church together, holding the key to the door— and to our future lives. I wear a simple, cream-colored, lacy dress; it isn't a wedding dress, just a beautiful dress Gerry saw in a store window one day and told me about. I'm wearing the gold locket Mom wore when she married Dad and carrying a simple bouquet of pink roses.

We have deliberately arrived early, long before anyone else. The aroma of long-past potluck lunches permeates the air in the little chapel, and I recall the families I once fellowshipped with here; it seems a lifetime ago. Together, Gerry and I stand at the front of the sanctuary, face each other, join hands, and bow our heads to pray. This time, we both want to do things right; we want God's blessing on our union from the very beginning. After we pray we slip out of the sanctuary and wait for the guests and the pastor to arrive.

Later, a woman we know from church plays a simple song on the piano at the front of the sanctuary, and Gerry and I enter again through the back door. We walk down the aisle together. As we near the front of the sanctuary, I glance over at the front pew where three handsome young men stand: Michael, and Gerry's sons, Brandon and Todd. After the ceremony these three young men will sign the register as witnesses to our union. Todd is not quite old enough to be a legal witness, but we want his signature to be there with the others. When we reach the front, we face the pastor. The piano music stops, and the pastor invites everyone to be seated and asks Gerry and me to turn toward one another. As we join hands, Gerry looks at me, winks, and grins.

In a few minutes, I will be part of another family.

Family Tree

Jerry and I settle into married life, and I'm happy. But even in that contentment, I still feel the need to fill in the gaps in my knowledge of my original family. With the increasing popularity and availability of information on the Internet, everyone, it seems, is researching their family tree; I'm no exception. I Google names and search for information about the Brauers and the Sellsteds. Armed with the little bit of information I have about my birth family, I try to piece together a biological family history. On Ancestry.com I discover I'm not the only one researching the history of the Letkeman family, and one day, as a lark, I post a request: "I am looking for information about a Mary Letkeman."

A few days later, I receive a response from a woman named Esther Zaccharias: "I have information about Mary Letkeman. But, my dear, which one are you interested in?"

I write back and explain that I was adopted and I am looking for the Mary Letkeman who was born in Kelstern, Saskatchewan, on April 8, 1919. Esther answers the next day: "You and I are kin. There is no doubt."

Esther Zacharias is my second cousin; my grandfather was the brother of her grandmother. We begin to correspond regularly and become e-mail friends. We learn we have much in common—our faith, a love of quilting, and a tendency toward depression. In her I find a confidante and a kindred spirit.

She sends me a family-history book that had been compiled for a reunion a number of years ago, though she cautions me it isn't entirely accurate. I'm thrilled to have pictures of my ancestors and information about where they came from in my hands. As I did with the library books I checked out when I first learned about my Mennonite heritage, I pore over the grainy photographs looking for facial features that will tangibly link me to Esther's family. I read the family stories, noting connections between names and the branches of the family tree as I try to piece together the history of my tribe.

Tucked inside the front cover of the book is a handwritten genealogy Esther has put together for me that dates back to the birth of Jacob Letkeman in 1685 in Altendorf, Prussia—my seventh great-grandfather! There are also photocopied pictures of Esther and her husband and their children and grandchildren. She's a kind-looking woman with hair the color of fresh snow. I find myself wishing I'd grown up knowing her.

Cousin Esther is doing extensive research for a book on our family genealogy. She hasn't completed it but has enough to satisfy my immediate curiosity. My family tree has deep roots and is rich with tradition and faith.

The first of the clan to come to Canada was a hard-working Russian Mennonite named Heinrich Letkeman, our great-grandfather. With his wife, Katarina, and their four children, he joined the mass migration of Mennonite Brethren from Osterwick, Russia, to Canada in 1876. Sadly, the voyage cost the life of their five-year-old son, who succumbed to illness before the six-week journey ended.

In Canada, the Letkemans settled in a Manitoba Mennonite community and joined with others to establish the first Mennonite Brethren church in Canada. Over the next six years, Katarina gave birth to four children, none of whom survived beyond their third birthday. Even the one son who survived the Atlantic crossing died within four years of their arrival. Sustained by their faith, the couple persevered and eventually had four more healthy children.

Scandal touched the family when Heinrich's youngest unmarried daughter, also named Katarina, became pregnant. Heinrich was angry and ashamed of his daughter's recklessness and when the time came for her to deliver her baby, he refused to allow medical help to be summoned. He considered her suffering payment for her sin. Young Katarina did not survive the birth, and her baby girl was given to a nearby family. Perhaps this baby girl was the first adoptee in the family. Heinrich's wife was heartbroken by the loss of her daughter and granddaughter and passed away a few months later.

My branch of the tree sprouted from Heinrich's youngest son, Jacob J. Letkeman, the *J* meant to distinguish him from the rest of the long line of Jacobs in the family. By all accounts, Jacob was a fine Christian man. He and his wife, Maria, had a son and three daughters. The youngest was named Katie, perhaps in honor of Jacob's deceased sister, Katarina. The family lived a quiet life, continuing the Mennonite homesteading tradition in Saskatchewan.

The second-youngest child of Jacob and Maria was Mary, my birth mother. Like all Jacob's children, Mary was educated at Bible school. She ended her education after eighth grade and went to work as a housekeeper. The rest of the story I already know.

I can't help but wonder if Mary heard stories about her grandfather's reaction to her aunt's out-of-wedlock pregnancy and felt his disapproval weigh heavily on her own shoulders. I think of my grandfather, Jacob, losing his sister so tragically, and I wonder if any of this contributed to Mary's decisions to give three of her children away. What would Jacob's reaction have been if he had known about Mary's pregnancies?

Cousin Esther encourages me to write something about Mary for her book. There is, of course, nothing about Wendy or me in the book yet nor even the fact that Donald is really Mary's child. Without my contribution the book will perpetuate the falsehood surrounding us and the truth will remain hidden. I wonder what kind of piece I could write about the woman who gave birth to four children, all, I assume, with different fathers. It is not my intention to cause angst to anyone, and when it comes time for me to sit down and write Mary's story, I find I can't.

Esther's book is printed without my piece, but she graciously includes information about me and sets the record straight about Donald's parentage. Although some of the details about me are not documented correctly—the book indicates I was adopted as a toddler—with the printing of Esther's book I finally have a documented genealogy.

One day, Esther and I correspond back and forth about Merlin and Donald. Since she has done so much genealogical research, I wonder if she has news about where they are and what they are doing; I haven't heard from Donald since our initial meeting at The Pantry and from Merlin since the day he met Wendy. I am stunned when she responds that she heard that

Merlin died. Using the Internet, I am able to confirm that he did indeed die a few years earlier; I even manage to locate his obituary.

I suppose there was no reason for anyone to have notified me about his death, just as there was no reason for anyone to have notified me when my Aunt Esther passed away a few years earlier. I am family and yet I am not.

Regardless of Merlin's apparent rejection of me, I feel compelled to acknowledge his passing, so I purchase a sympathy card, write a brief note, and put it in the mail to Sandy. I expect nothing from her in return; it just seems like the right thing to do.

Another Family Farewell

*I*ve forgotten how cold December in Saskatchewan can be. Given a choice, as much as I love my prairie home province, I wouldn't choose to come in winter. But Myra phoned on Christmas Day to tell me Uncle Albert was found dead in the cab of his pickup truck, the victim of a sudden heart attack.

Gerry and I arrive at Uncle Bill's house first and settle into one of the guest rooms. He seems polite, though somewhat distant. I assume he's working through the shock of Uncle Albert's death. Lori and her fiancé arrive the following day. I haven't seen her since Mom died sixteen years ago, and we only talked briefly when Aunt Edie died four years ago. I'm apprehensive about seeing her but also hopeful; I can't help but wonder if our relationship can change now that we are both older.

The first morning after we're all there, Lori and I sip coffee and talk in the living room, dancing warily around each other. I think we're both hoping we can build a relationship again but are so different that it's hard to find common ground aside from the fact that we grew up in the same home.

That afternoon Lori and I go with Uncle Bill to Uncle Albert's house in Benson. His absence falls over me like a shroud as we step out of the frigid afternoon into the shelter of the chilly kitchen. I am taken back in time.

When Lori and I were children, we begged Mom and Dad to let us stay with Grandma and Uncle Albert for a few extra days after a family visit. Uncle Albert promised to bring us back to Moose Jaw.

I remember Grandma feeding us cookies for breakfast and mixing the capsule of yellow coloring into the white oleo to make a spread for our sandwiches at lunchtime. We rode in the back of Uncle Albert's pickup truck over hot, dusty roads to the farm. He taught us how to chew grain to make gum. He took us for rides on his tractor, and when he went out to work in the fields, we played on the sunporch, pretending a tornado was coming when the wind picked up. I remember Uncle Albert's particular way of saying "warshed" instead of "washed" and the way he always said "hey?" before answering a question.

Today the tiny table in the kitchen is spread with paperwork; Uncle Bill has already started the task of sorting through records. The business of death supersedes the desire to be still and reflect on a life that has come to an end. In my mind it's more than a life that has come to an end; it's a family. Grandma and her three children are all gone; only Lori and I remain.

I am touched to find school pictures of Laurinda and Michael propped up on the wall next to the table in the front room. But I'm surprised when Uncle Bill leans in for a closer look and comments, "I don't know who they are."

We step into the tiny room where Grandma slept with Mom and Aunt Edie when they were children. I remember sleeping with Grandma in the big bed, while Lori slept in a tiny bed that was in the room that one time we stayed with them. I remember the sheer, off-white curtains blowing in a welcome breeze. I can still hear the tick tock of the white clock that once sat on the dresser next to the framed black-and-white picture of Mom as a young woman.

"Is there anything you want to take with you?" Uncle Bill asks.

All of it—I want all of it, I want to tell him. It's all that is left of my childhood, and I don't want to let anything go. Lori asks for the sign with Uncle Albert's name on it that is tacked to the front of the house. I reach for a crude oil painting of the Benson elevator; the signature is a neighbor's whose name I recognize.

"Where is the picture of Mom?" I ask.

"Oh, the frame was broken." Uncle Bill says. "I have the photograph at home."

I find it odd that Uncle Bill would take the photograph of Mom home with him, and I ask to have it when we get back to his house, promising Lori that I will have a copy made and send it to her.

———

On the day of the funeral, Lori and I walk down the aisle toward the front of the drafty old Lutheran church. Each step leaves a satisfactory thunk on the old wooden floor like a somber percussion accompaniment to the organ. The low moan of the frigid prairie wind outside completes the woeful ensemble. Neither of us is dressed adequately for the Saskatchewan winter afternoon.

Once again the pews on each side are filled with faces I barely recognize. My gaze is fixed on the elaborate bronze casket at the front of the church. Its stark contrast with the simple farmer it contains is like a melody sung slightly off-key. Uncle Bill and Myra picked it out before we arrived and joked to me about how Uncle Albert would have hated the extravagance. Why did you choose it then? I wanted to say. I know Uncle Albert wouldn't have liked it, and I can't help but wonder if they were just trying to spend as much of his money as possible to prevent Lori and me from getting it. We're Uncle Albert's sole heirs.

As we draw closer to the casket, Uncle Albert's profile becomes visible. The face is that of the uncle I loved from childhood, but the spirit of that man is not there. Heavy pancake makeup coats his face to cover the effects of being in his truck for twenty-four hours before he was found, and I find myself wondering morbidly what twenty-four hours outside in extreme frigid temperature does to a body. His large, rugged hands are crossed over his chest, and the top one hovers ever so slightly above the lower, as if still frozen in place.

Beside me, Lori begins to sniffle, and I reach over and guide her to our place in the family pew. I sit between Uncle Bill and Gerry, and Lori takes her place on the other side of Uncle Bill, next to her fiancé.

The minister enters the sanctuary, the nondescript organ music changes to the old familiar hymn "Softly and Tenderly," and the congregation stands, hymnals in hand, and begins to sing. Again the words of the refrain "come home, come home" tug on my heart and remind me that this place will always be the home of my heart.

When the Lutheran minister who is doing the service asked if I would like to read a passage at the funeral, I didn't wait for him to suggest one; this time I told the minister what I wanted to read. When the time comes, I stand in my black dress, step up to the podium, and look out over the congregation for a moment before opening my Bible to the passage I've chosen.

But I do not want you to be ignorant, brethren, concerning those who have fallen asleep, lest you sorrow as others who have no hope. For if we believe that Jesus died and rose again, even so God will bring with Him those who sleep in Jesus.

For this we say to you by the word of the Lord, that we who were alive and remain until the coming of the Lord will by no means precede those who were asleep. For the Lord Himself will descend from heaven with a shout, with the voice of an archangel, and with the trumpet of God. And the dead in Christ will rise first. Then we who were alive and remain shall be caught up together with them in the clouds to meet the Lord in the air. And thus we shall always be with the Lord. Therefore comfort one another with these words." (1 Thess. 4:13-18)

I close my Bible and look out over the congregation as I read the last sentence.

After all of the hymns are sung, the scripture read, and the eulogy given, the minister steps down from the platform. Six men stand, don heavy coats, and take their places to carry the casket down the aisle. When they pass our pew, we take our place behind them, and with slow steady steps, our little procession makes its way toward the back of the chapel.

In the foyer the wooden doors whine as the ushers push them open, allowing the howling wind to enter the sanctuary. Two elderly war veterans serve as an honor guard and salute as Uncle Albert is carried into the frigid afternoon toward the waiting hearse.

Family Bible

few months later, Gerry and I are about to leave for Saskatchewan again for the farm auction of Uncle Albert's estate. I'm surprised when Uncle Bill calls and tells me we won't be able to stay at his house because his nephew Floyd from Regina will be staying there. There was plenty of room when Aunt Edie died, and when Uncle Albert died there was room for Gerry and me as well as Lori and her fiancé. I sense that something is amiss but cordially agree that we'll check into the local motel.

We arrive the day before the auction. After checking into the motel, we go to the diner. Coincidentally Lori and her fiancé are there. We sit down with them at a chrome and Formica table, and Lori immediately tells us that something is wrong.

"Brian and I ran into Uncle Bill when we got here a couple of hours ago," she says. "He seemed mad about something."

"Why would he be mad?" I ask her, assuming she must have misinterpreted him.

While we are talking, Uncle Bill and Floyd come in. They don't see us and sit down at a table across the room. I walk over to greet them. Though I didn't know Floyd when I was younger, I got to know him at the funerals of Aunt Edie and Uncle Albert, and he has always been amicable to me.

"Gerry and I are sitting over here with Lori and Brian," I tell Uncle Bill. "Would you join us?"

He doesn't acknowledge the group I left at the table and just looks straight ahead at Floyd. "We're waiting for someone," he says gruffly.

And in that moment I know Lori is right. I have no idea what's caused this apparent shunning. Uncle Bill asks gruffly if we want to go out to Uncle Albert's place after we eat; there are some personal family things that the auction people have left there for us to go through before the sale. Of course I say we do.

At Uncle Albert's house—under the watchful eye of Uncle Bill—we climb the steep stairs to the attic. When I was a child, the door at the top of the stairs was boarded closed, I suppose in an attempt to keep the temperature downstairs stabilized in the oppressive Saskatchewan summer heat and the unbearable frigid winters. The steps were only used to store sacks of flour and potatoes. It's exciting to ascend those dark wooden steps now. As a child I suspected there were hidden treasures in the attic, and now I'm about to find out.

There is nothing of monetary worth in the dark attic, but the treasures we find are priceless to me for what they reveal of the harsh lives of those I loved who grew up in this little house. Lori and I sit on the floor, opening boxes and trunks that haven't been opened for years. We exclaim over things like coal-oil lamps, fur muffs, photographs, schoolbooks with Mom's handwriting (beautiful even when she was a child), claiming things for ourselves that catch our interest. In an attempt to keep the fragile peace between us, I defer to Lori when we find something we both want, and I take time to point out the names of people in photographs; as the older sister, I have a stronger recollection of people and places than she does.

Two oval, tortoiseshell frames hold portraits of young men in World War I uniforms. I know they are the Graves boys, Grandma's brothers who perished in World War I. George Riddell Graves was eighteen and Richard Albert Graves, twenty-seven. Gerry suggests we try to find the boys' families so we can send the pictures to them. I bristle.

"They were *my* family."

From deep within an old trunk I lift out a stack of fabric and quilt squares, many of them pieced from a rough checked fabric that I suspect was once part of a pair of overalls or a shirt. Others are pieced with fabric in red and white stripes combined with a blue and white polka-dotted and patterned fabric reminiscent of the 1930s. The stitching is rough and utilitarian. I picture Grandma on a cold winter evening sitting by the window to get more light, piecing the squares together. I wonder if she took pleasure in the task or if it was just one more chore that had to be done. I claim the quilt squares for my own.

When we're finished looking through everything in the attic, we descend the steep stairs and Uncle Bill directs us to a few more boxes that are sitting on the tiny kitchen table. From one of them I lift a Bible, the front cover held together with silver duct tape. I smile to think of Uncle Albert patching the well-worn book.

The front cover and the first few pages are filled with names and dates written in a beautiful cursive script. It's a family Bible! Lori expresses no interest in keeping it, and I hug it to my chest, eager to look through the names when I'm alone.

Later that evening, when Gerry and I are back in our drafty motel room, I settle down to look at the Bible more closely. Tucked throughout the pages are cards announcing deaths and funerals of family members and friends from the 1800s to the present. There are little handouts from the funerals of Grandma, Aunt Edie, Mom, and Dad, pressed flowers saved from one occasion or another, and newspaper clippings with obituary notices.

I flip to the front pages. The writing, I now realize, is in different hands, as the Bible was passed down over the years. There are birth dates and death dates for names I recognize and for others I don't. I even find the names and dates of birth and death for the Graves boys. I turn the pages gently, awed at holding such a treasure in my hand. I recognize my grandma's handwriting in the birth dates of Mom, Aunt Edie, and Uncle Albert, and the dates that Mom and Aunt Edie were married. Uncle Albert's handwriting records the dates his mother and his younger sisters died.

But something is missing from this family record, and I go back through the pages once more in a vain attempt to find it. There is no record of Lori and me or of Laurinda and Michael. I am stunned to realize that no one documented our names as part of the family's history. Was it because we were adopted?

It must have been Grandma who chose not to include us. But we're her only grandchildren. Did she really not consider us part of the family? I remember her indifference to us as children. I thought it was just her way; I never imagined it was because she didn't regard us as her granddaughters. I pick up a pen and consider adding us to the record. Instead, in my very best handwriting, I record Uncle Albert's name and death date; then I close the book.

The next afternoon, Gerry takes the familiar turnoff at the white church steeple onto the road that leads into Benson. I've never been to an estate auction before and have no idea what to expect. Judging from the number of vehicles lining the streets and parked in empty lots in the tiny hamlet, it's a big occasion.

A flock of buyers has come out on this warm April afternoon to bid on pieces of my family. Gerry finds a place to park, and we walk down the muddy street toward Uncle Albert's Quonset, a large semicircular structure made of corrugated galvanized steel. Directly adjacent to the Quonset, in what is normally an empty field, is an assortment of tractors, trucks, cars, all-terrain vehicles, a combine, and other farm implements I recognize by sight but don't know the names of. I'm astounded by the sheer volume of equipment my uncle owned. I'm pleased, too, especially when I think about him growing up during the Great Depression with no father, working hard, and ultimately achieving financial security and prosperity.

Uncle Bill is sitting at a picnic table, Floyd is standing next to him, and they are talking to a man wearing a cap that says "Hodgins Auctioneers." We walk over to them, and after the auctioneer walks away, I greet my uncle.

"Hi, Uncle Bill. How are you feeling today?"

He grunts a response and turns toward Floyd. I'm immediately confused; why does he seem angry with me? I want to ask him if I've offended him, but I don't want to disturb him on this day that must be difficult for him as well. Perhaps there will be a better time later.

I hear the squeal of a microphone and see the auctioneer standing on top of a scaffold-like structure with a handful of papers in his hand. The auction is about to begin. I see Lori and her fiancé in the field where the farm implements are, and Gerry and I wander to watch the bidding with them.

"Are you going to bid on anything?" I ask her.

It seems surreal that Lori and I would have to bid on anything we wanted when we are the sole heirs to the estate, but that's what Uncle Bill, as executor, had decided.

"Maybe," Lori responds. "I would like to have his truck."

Lori, despite her tough exterior, has a soft heart, and I know it would mean a lot to her to drive Uncle Albert's truck. The bidding is fast; these farmers know what they came for and what everything is worth. I'm pleased when they get to Uncle Albert's pickup truck and Lori's bid is the winning one.

"Congratulations!" I tell her as she grins widely.

There are still many pieces of equipment to auction off, but I decide to leave the group and head over to the yard around the house where the smaller household items are being auctioned off at the same time; I'm more interested in these personal items.

I recognize Floyd's son standing in front of the podium; he's a tall man wearing an Australian walkabout hat. It seems bizarre to watch strangers bid on dishes and furniture I remember from my childhood. How it is possible that Grandma's old Singer treadle sewing machine is for sale and no one asked me if I wanted it first? I suppose I could bid on it, but the thought of bidding on my own grandmother's sewing machine is so distasteful that I dismiss it immediately, a decision I will later regret.

As I am listening to the bidding and the good-natured banter between the auctioneer and the bidders, Myra walks into the yard. She strides purposefully past me toward Floyd's son and slaps him firmly on the shoulder in greeting; they laugh together at something one of the bidders has said.

I am thankful for my dark sunglasses. Even though Myra isn't a biological relative, she has lived in this area all her life and is treated like part of the family. I'm the outsider being purposely ignored for a reason I can't fathom.

After all the household goods and farm equipment are sold, it's time to auction Uncle Albert's three parcels of farmland and the tiny house in Benson. Lori and I were both given the opportunity to keep the Benson property, and Gerry and I have discussed it at length. My propensity to be drawn to place made me want to hang on to the little house where Mom grew up; it holds so many rich memories from my childhood and so much of my family history. But we agree that my desire is more sentimental than practical, and we have no use for the property. Even though Saskatchewan is the home of my heart, it's unlikely we will come back very often now that Aunt Edie and Uncle Albert are gone.

I stand at the back of the community center where the land auction is taking place and see Uncle Bill sitting near the front with Floyd and Myra. Though Lori and I are the beneficiaries of Uncle Albert's will, as executor of the estate he has the right to decline a final bid that he deems too low. From my vantage point, he seems puffed up with importance, almost demanding respect.

Bidding goes quickly, and I'm touched by two young men, obviously just starting out as farmers, who confer again and again as they bid. I want them to have the land. I want it to go to a family just starting out. I want to know it will care for another family the way it cared for mine. In the end, though, the bidding goes too high, and the young men drop out. The land goes to a local man, and as the gavel is banged on the table to finalize the sale, I hear rumblings of distrust for this individual. He's buying up large parcels in the area. It's the way of the future, it seems.

After the land is sold, all that's left is the tiny house in Benson. At first, there are no hands raised in response to the auctioneer's opening bid. He lowers the price once, twice, three times, and still no hands are raised. I want to raise my hand; I want the house. I turn and step outside, barely able to stop myself from bidding on my grandma's house.

I step back into the community center in time to see a local man bid successfully; he gets the property and house for a mere $6,000.

Paternal Family

The auction leaves me feeling bruised and bleeding. Uncle Bill is my last connection to the family I grew up with, and I feel inexplicably and totally alienated from him. Gerry suggests I write him a letter or call and ask what caused this rift, but I'm afraid to risk further rejection. I send him Christmas cards and letters for a couple of years, but he never responds.

I immerse myself in my work, still searching for a sense of significance wherever I can find it. I'm bolstered by the sense of doing a job well and contributing in a meaningful way to something, even if it's a corporation instead of an extended family. On the outside it appears that my life is full and rich, and in many ways it is.

Gerry and I enjoy Sunday dinners with whichever of our children can make it each week. Brandon marries, and I gain another daughter. Nicole is smart, beautiful, generous, and loving. I am proud to consider her family and enjoy getting to know her. The following year, Laurinda marries Gord, and he wins my heart the moment I see tears falling down his face as he watches his beautiful bride cross the little garden bridge toward him. Michael comes to live with Gerry and me for a while when he goes back to school, and my heart warms as I watch the two of them banter back and forth at the dinner table each evening. We learn Internet chat as we connect with Todd, who takes an extended trip to Australia after he finishes high school.

I exchange infrequent e-mails and phone calls with Lori, but our relationship remains uneasy. Wendy moves to Korea to teach English, and more and more time passes between our e-mails. Only my cousin Esther Zacharias remains a constant in my life; my e-mail relationship with her is my only connection to my tribe.

There is still a void in me. Once I thought that if I could learn the truth about my heritage, I'd feel complete, and to a certain extent, I do feel more settled since connecting with my birth mother's family. But I'm still struggling to feel worthy and connected.

My mother's family is only part of the puzzle, and eventually, when I can't ignore the void any longer, I contact the Saskatchewan Post-Adoption Division once more to see if they can help me locate my paternal family. Maybe if I can fill in that missing piece, I will begin to feel whole at last.

One afternoon a phone call comes from Saskatchewan, strikingly similar to the one I got many years ago from Walter Andres. This time there's a woman on the other end of the line. She introduces herself as Bev Jaigobin—another name that is immediately burned into my memory. She has located my paternal family, has just spoken with a man who is my half brother, and has discovered that I have four more half siblings.

I scramble to find notepaper and a pen and scribble notes as she talks.

My birth father was born in 1913 and died at sixty-eight. Bev has spoken to my half brother Frank; at sixty-nine, he is twenty-four years my senior, six feet tall, weighs 180 pounds, and has gray hair that was once red. He lives in Campbell River, British Columbia. My next-oldest brother, Ed, died of a heart attack four years earlier when he was sixty-two. Next in line is my half sister Miriam, eleven years older than me, married with one son. The youngest sister is Ruth, nine years older than me and, according to Bev, ecstatic to learn about me. Bev gives me my brother Frank's phone number and tells me he is expecting my call at six o'clock that evening.

I'm not surprised to learn my birth father has already died—he would be ninety-one if he were alive. I'm more surprised by the ages of my new brothers, though I guess I shouldn't be. After we hang up, I jot down some questions I want to ask Frank. What is the family's nationality? What was the cause of our father's death? What was his name? Can I contact my sisters? What about pictures? This time, I will ask for pictures.

I sit at the kitchen table with knots in my stomach as the numbers on the clock move from 5:45 to 6:00.

"This is Linda," I say when he answers the phone.

"Well hello!" he chuckles. "This is all certainly a surprise!"

He is friendly and welcoming as he tells me about our father. "His name was Francis—he was called Frank, like me. He was living in Moose Jaw when he died. I think it was a heart problem," Frank says. "He had no family around him; he could be verbally abusive, but I understand he had good friends from his church."

This doesn't sound good.

"I don't know much about his family history other than the fact that there is a relative named Gideon Mosher who was a Quaker from Pennsylvania."

He tells me about his niece Cindy, our brother Ed's daughter who is compiling a family history, and gives me her e-mail address. "She'll be able to give you all that kind of information."

He tells me about his siblings—our siblings.

"Well, Ed died of a heart attack; that's the only health issue I'm aware of in the family. Miriam is pretty easygoing, and Ruth likes music. Ruth is very excited to talk to you and meet you," he tells me. By the end of our conversation, I have Ruth's phone number in my hand and encouragement from Frank to phone her. In fact, he says, she's waiting for a call from me tonight.

Ruth sounds happy but nervous when I talk to her, and she promises to e-mail me some photographs right away. This time the information exchange is much quicker than the one with my maternal family almost twenty years earlier. We have the benefit of instant contact via e-mail, and within days Ruth sends me pictures of my brothers and sisters.

I don't have the same gut reaction at seeing the faces of people who are related to me this time. My brothers are much older and I don't see any resemblance between them and me. I can see few similarities between Ruth's features and mine, but I'm startled when I see the picture of Miriam. I feel like I'm looking in a mirror. Her blonde hair is styled much like mine, her cheekbones are prominent like mine, and her eyes seem to be my eyes.

———

Ruth and I get to know one another over the next couple of years via e-mail and an occasional telephone conversation. My niece Cindy and I exchange e-mails. She sends pictures of her four children and their families and fills me in on much of the family history. She is preparing a family genealogy and asks my permission to include information about me and my family. I'm happy to be included. Muriel, Cindy's mother and my brother Ed's wife, telephones me now and then and is welcoming and friendly. She too is adopted and with Cindy's help was recently reunited with her birth family.

Gerry and I are planning to be on vacation near Medicine Hat, where Ruth and Miriam live, in the following September, 2005, and we make plans to meet in person. As I watch the prairie landscape go by and we get closer to Medicine Hat, I find myself in a state of déjà vu. What if they don't like me? I ask myself, just as I did before I met Wendy for the first time. Back then it didn't occur to me to wonder whether I would like her; I had assumed that the power to make or break the new sister relationship rested entirely with her. Now I'm older and more secure, so I consider both questions.

I close my eyes and offer up a quick prayer as Gerry pulls into the parking lot of the A&W, where we have agreed to meet. I'm not certain if I'm about to meet one sister or two; when I spoke to Ruth last, she wasn't sure if Miriam would be coming. In this family, too, there seems to be one individual who might not be able to handle learning about another sister.

As I open the car door, a woman comes out of the restaurant, and I take a deep breath.

Ruth is smiling expectantly as she walks toward us. Her graying hair is cut short and her eyes are smiling behind her glasses. She is dressed casually in pants and a white sweater; she looks like her picture, except her smile is wider.

"Linda?" I can tell she is nervous; shyness seems to run on both sides of my family.

"Yes. Ruth?" I laugh, and we embrace.

"I'm so happy to finally meet you!" she says as she looks into my face. "Miriam is waiting for us inside."

"Oh, she came! I'm so glad!"

I recognize my sister as soon as we walk into the restaurant. She sits alone at a table, and her gaze turns our way as we walk toward her. She too is dressed casually and wears a yellow T-shirt underneath a light brown jacket. There is something about her that haunts me. Miriam's face reflects my own, though she's a bit heavier than me. Her demeanor is hesitant; she doesn't rise, and we don't embrace.

"Hi, Miriam," I say as we join her at the table. Frank and Ruth didn't tell Miriam about me right away. She has been struggling with depression, and they were concerned with how she might react. As recently as the day before, Ruth says, she wasn't sure if Miriam would join us.

Ruth sits next to her, and Gerry and I sit across from them. There is nervous laughter from all of us. I reach under the table and rest my hand on Gerry's leg, thankful for the touchstone to my reality. Miriam speaks haltingly, the effect, I assume, of the shock treatment Ruth told me she's had to treat her deep depression.

Depression seems to be part of my maternal and paternal families. Perhaps part of my own experience of depression was due to a genetic predisposition.

I'm uncomfortable with Miriam. She looks a lot like me but seems haunted and hurt beyond my reach. I silently grieve over the loss of this sister I am unlikely ever to really know.

In contrast, Ruth is bubbly and welcoming, her shyness much like my own, making her talk nervously.

"We have pictures, if you would like to see them," she says, sensitive to how I might be feeling at this moment. She passes around pictures of Miriam and herself as children and others of Frank and Ed. There's such a large age difference between the girls and boys that it's almost as if there are two families.

Finally she hands me one a single one and says, "And this is our father."

The face in the photograph is rough, unshaven, and unattractive.

"What was he like?" I ask, trying to ignore the lump in my stomach and my discomfort at seeing his face.

"He was mean," Miriam responds immediately.

As we talk and I learn more about the man who is my birth father, I am again filled with gratitude for the family I grew up in. It seems that growing up with my birth father would have been even worse than growing up with my birth mother.

By all accounts, Francis Wilmot Mosher was a bitter and angry man. Frank, as he was known, made his living as a farmer until 1972, when he moved to a one-room apartment in Moose Jaw and cut off all contact with his wife and children. He must have been lonely, separated from his family as he was. Over the years he sometimes wrote to his daughters Ruth and Miriam, and perhaps also to Frank and Ed, but the letters he wrote didn't express any affection. They were full of harsh words about other family members—the sort of words intended to bring division. Even in his reaching out, his selfishness superseded any attempt to be a father.

When his children were young, he refused to provide financial support, even when the need was great and the children had medical expenses. This forced Frank and Ed to work to provide for Miriam, Ruth, and their mother. He also refused to step up to his role as father. At one point Miriam ran wild and her mother contacted Frank senior to ask for help. He refused.

He was a bitter man, unfaithful to his wife, and he gossiped about each of his family members, spreading tales. Even after his death he rejected his family. He left a token amount to each of the four children, nothing to his wife, and the bulk of his estate to his church in Moose Jaw. While I'm glad to know that this vindictive man may have found friends and a home of sorts in his church, and I hope he found peace before he died, it angers me that he never felt compelled to mend the wounds he'd inflicted on his wife and children.

Unknowingly, he left a gift for me, his forgotten and unacknowledged daughter. As I learn more about the character of my birth father, I resolve anew to live a life of meaning and purpose that will be remembered differently than his. In no way do I want to be remembered as my father's daughter.

Two Hearts

For you formed my inward parts;
You covered me in my mother's womb.
I will praise You, for I am fearfully and wonderfully made;
marvelous are Your works,
and that my soul knows very well.
My frame was not hidden from You, when I was made in secret,
and skillfully wrought in the lowest parts of the earth.
Your eyes saw my substance, being yet unformed.
And in Your book they were all written, the days fashioned for me,
when as yet there were none of them. (Psalm 139:13-16)

The Trunk

One day out of the blue, I receive a small card in the mail from Sandy, Merlin's widow. She says she misplaced the condolence card I sent when I learned of Merlin's passing, and only found it again recently. She wants me to have the infamous trunk that Merlin kept after our mother died. I'm stunned. After all this time, I can find out what secrets are hidden in the trunk. I call her immediately.

She tells me about Merlin's quick decline and sudden death from pancreatic cancer and about her subsequent years of grief. She tells me about Chelsey, their late-in-life daughter, and how much she would like to meet Auntie Linda. She is friendly, almost pushy, wanting to get together and wanting her daughter, my niece, to get to know me.

"The trunk contains some handwork your mother did, her wedding dress, and some pictures. It also contains some things that were yours," she tells me.

I feel pressured. It's too late, I want to tell her. Despite my curiosity to learn what the trunk contains, I put her off, telling her I'm busy with my job and will call in a week or two to make arrangements for us to get together.

It's more than a year before I contact her again. I could say I was busy with work and life, and that would be true, but the more accurate truth is that I wasn't ready to hold in my hands things that had belonged to my birth mother and to learn the trunk's secrets. I got a reprieve when I first contacted my birth family and learned that Mary had already passed away; I was spared the emotion of meeting the woman who gave me life and then gave me up. For all these years, the grainy black-and-white photographs of her were enough. I'm also resentful of Sandy. I wonder if she is partly to blame that my brother and I didn't have a relationship. I suppose part of me is even jealous of the time she had with Merlin and Mary.

When I e-mail Sandy to let her know Gerry is going to be in Vancouver visiting Todd and will pick up the trunk, she seems disappointed we won't have an opportunity to get together. I'm just relieved to be spared the drama of a reunion; it's become clear to me that it's more important to me to know about my family of origin than to actually be part of it.

Between my initial conversation with Sandy and the time we make arrangements to get the trunk, Gerry and I move to Washington State. The home we purchase is larger than our home in Kamloops and, though I love it, the rooms echo with emptiness. I miss Sunday dinners with our children, and the laughter and good-natured teasing that permeated our dining room walls when Michael or Todd or Brandon was there. I miss the living room where I stood with Laurinda and adjusted her wedding veil. I miss friends, sunshine, and the familiarity of the city where I spent most of my life.

But things change, time moves on, and Gerry and I are happy creating a different life in Washington. Brandon and Nicole now live in Calgary, as do Laurinda and Gord. Todd is making a home for himself in Vancouver. Only Michael remains in Kamloops, and he sometimes talks about moving elsewhere. As much as I would like to have family around, it seems it's not to be.

———◆———

On a hot August afternoon, Gerry brings home the blue steamer trunk that has traveled across miles and through time to get to me. He puts it down on the hardwood floor in our front foyer. It's small—certainly not large enough to hold our mother's body, as Wendy and I once irreverently joked.

It's rectangular in shape with a blue vinyl exterior and brass corners. It resembles a similar trunk that is stored in my attic and holds keepsakes I treasure: Mom's wedding dress, Dad's army uniform, love letters from Dad to Mom, Mom's sealskin fur coat, family pictures, baby clothes worn by me and Laurinda and Michael, and at the very bottom, two guest books and two bundles of sympathy cards from Mom's and Dad's funerals.

"I'll open it later," I tell Gerry, pretending to be busy with household duties.

But the small blue trunk lures me, and after about a half hour I can't resist any longer. I kneel in front of it and lift the latches, taking a deep breath before lifting the heavy lid. The scent of mothballs and secrets wafts up as I raise the cover, revealing a tray strewn with newspaper clippings that describe events I know nothing about and people I don't recognize. There's a tiny wedding picture, and I recognize Mary's face; behind her glasses, her eyes appear to be squinting toward the camera. I set it aside to look at more closely later, frustrated at seeing yet another picture in which I can't clearly see her eyes.

I lift the top tray out of the trunk and set it aside, revealing various pieces of linens embroidered with flowers and swirls; this must be the hand-work that Sandy mentioned. For a moment I rest my hand on an embroidered flower, imagining the hand of my birth mother touching the same place sometime in the past.

There's a book with recipes clipped from newspapers tucked between the handwritten pages, and I pause. This must be Mary's writing. It's foreign to me, nothing like Mom's cursive script on the cards and letters tucked away in my larger trunk in the attic. One look at Mom's handwriting is enough to send me on a trip back to my childhood; this handwriting is unfamiliar and unattractive.

There's a large scrapbook with clippings of poems, songs, and Bible verses. A handmade construction-paper booklet contains drawings of houses and clocks that look like a study in perspective. At the top of one sheet, written in pencil in a childish script, is her name and grade: Mary Letkeman, Grade VIII. Underneath that I find a school record with her name on it; apparently school wasn't her strong suit.

A musty mothball scent threatens to overcome me despite the shallow breaths I'm taking, but I continue to sift through the items and find a wedding dress. I remember the fun I used to have trying on Mom's wedding dress when I was a child; the thought of putting this dress on fills me with revulsion. I'm still harboring anger toward Mary. I lift the dress out—not even bothering to hold it up to see what it looks like—and set it aside.

I find another yellowed newspaper, this one folded with the obituary page on top. Mary's name jumps out at me. It's her obituary: "Mary was predeceased by her husband and is survived by her sisters and one son." One son? What about the rest of us? Bitterly, I set the yellowed newspaper aside.

I find Merlin's school pictures and books that must have been his as a child. There are pictures of Merlin with Donald, two cousin-brothers, playing together. I wonder if his unusual family situation is part of the reason it seems Donald hasn't found his place in life yet. Sandy told me that Donald had lived with her and Merlin for a time and that Merlin was trying to help him out. But something had happened that caused them to become estranged. I wonder if we all would have turned out to be different people if we'd grown up together.

The color pink catches my eye and I take out a box that contains a little pink hairbrush and comb. This must be the reason Merlin kept anyone from looking in the trunk; it contained evidence of a baby girl. Again I consider the impact on ten-year-old Merlin when his baby sister, Wendy, disappeared from the family, and I wonder what he was told had happened to her.

When Sandy told me there were things that belonged to me in the trunk, I didn't consciously realize that they must be Wendy's, not mine. Or perhaps I did, but chose not to acknowledge it. Perhaps some part of me wanted to find my own tangible connection to the woman who bore me. From a place in the trunk near the baby items, I lift a cardboard picture holder. The face of a beautiful baby—Wendy—looks back at me. How could Mary have cared for this angelic baby and voluntarily given her up? As I look at the face of my baby sister I realize that this trunk doesn't belong to me at all; it belongs to Wendy.

I take a cursory look at the rest of the contents at the bottom of the trunk and am about to start putting everything back when something shiny in the bottom corner catches my eye.

Though the trunk and its contents belong rightfully to Wendy, I know without a doubt that this one shiny item is meant to be mine. It's a gold locket, just like the one I have that belonged to Mom. I hold the locket in my closed fist, take a few more pictures out of the trunk to look at later, and close the lid.

I'm drained as I lean on the trunk and stand up. I'm angry and feel left out. There is some evidence of each of Mary's children except me in the trunk. Once more, I feel forgotten and invisible.

Later, I show the locket to Gerry, and we compare it to Mom's. They're identical in size, shape, and color. Only the etchings on the front are different: Mary's heart bears the image of a second, smaller heart in the center.

"You will know that I'm healed from the past when I'm able to wear this locket," I tell Gerry as I tuck it far in the back corner of my dresser drawer.

I have no intention of ever putting it on.

Genesis

The cave you fear to enter holds the treasure you seek.

—JOSEPH CAMPBELL

Grandma's Visit

Spring 2009

Slowly, Laurinda opens the bedroom door, and we tiptoe inside the darkened room. A little head with tufts of red hair lifts from within the cherry wooden crib and turns toward us. Makiya's smile lights up her whole face, her eyes twinkle, and her little button nose crinkles just at the top. She looks at her mom and her smile grows larger. Then she turns slightly toward me, her smile never wavering for a second.

Laurinda has warned me that the five-month-old has started "making strange" around people recently. It's been over three months since my last visit, and she knows how much I've looked forward to seeing Makiya again; she doesn't want me to be surprised or disappointed if Makiya cries when she sees me at first. Smugly, I've assured her that Makiya knows her grandma and not to worry. It seems I'm right.

We lean over the crib and coo at the precious baby, who continues to look back and forth between us, smiling the whole time. Suddenly Makiya passes gas, and we both laugh.

"Oh, there's my rootin', tootin' girl," Laurinda jokes as she gently brushes Makiya's head with her hand.

"Hi, sweetie," I greet the beautiful girl. "It's Grandma! You remember Grandma, don't you?"

For a few moments we just stand and talk softly to Makiya, and she is content to listen to us chatter. Finally I can stand it no longer. "Laurinda, can I pick her up?"

Laurinda laughs. "Of course! I'll just grab a diaper, and we'll change her."

I reach into the crib and push back Makiya's quilt. Her little body is warm from her nap. As I lift her from the crib and pull her toward me, a blanket of peace embraces me and time seems to fall away. In the five months since Makiya was born, I have frequently found myself in a reflective state. I am five years younger than Mom was when she died and am starting to have a sense of my own mortality. I often think about the legacy I want to leave behind; my sense of purpose has started to shift.

I am proud of my daughter's transformation from daughter to mother. In some ways it seems only yesterday that I was a young mother and Mom had come to see baby Laurinda. Just as the relationship between Mom and me deepened and changed after I became a mother, so too has Laurinda's and mine. I hold Makiya closely and inhale that sweet baby scent from the crease in her neck as I reach up and smooth the red hair that has become mussed during her nap. What a surprise that red hair was when she was born, until I remembered that my brother Frank also had red hair. Laurinda had lots of hair when she was born, too, but hers was black and eventually turned blonde like mine. Hair surprises seem to run in the family.

Laurinda returns with the diaper and spreads a changing pad out on the bed. Reluctantly, I surrender Makiya and set her gently down. I watch Laurinda's slow and easy manner as she bends toward her precious daughter and removes the wet diaper. She chats with her constantly, encouraging her smiles. There is no sense of urgency or hurry in anything that she does. Now thirty, Laurinda has waited a long time for Makiya, and she is enjoying every second of being a mom.

Makiya stares up into her eyes, now and then glancing over toward me, but it's obvious that she truly has eyes only for her mommy. I am thankful that this precious five-month-old can rest in the love of her mommy.

I recently realized that it is almost exactly fifty years to the day when I was a five-month-old infant and met my own mommy and daddy for the first time. Even though I've learned the truth about my heritage, hidden just beneath the surface there is still a sense of rejection and shame. For some reason it has come up frequently in the past few months, and each time the pain surprises me.

I've started thinking about the months before I became Linda Gail Brauer. Who took care of me? I have always assumed that I was placed in a foster home. Did my foster parents miss me when I was adopted? In my imagination I see a young woman holding a baby, a husband's arms around her, both of them kissing a baby's head and inhaling that sweet baby smell. I see a few tears slide down the woman's cheeks even though she tries to hide them. I imagine that though she knew this day would come, it's harder than she expected it would be to let me go. Perhaps for months or even years afterward she keeps a picture of me on her mantle to remind herself of those precious few months when she cared for me.

On the other hand, maybe there was no young woman caring for me; maybe I really was in a crib in an institution along with other unwanted babies, just as the now-infamous chosen-baby story said. I push these thoughts aside, focus on the present, and enjoy my precious granddaughter.

The Last Good-bye

Summer 2009

I am in my backyard, gently swaying in the lawn swing, relaxing after work. My Yorkie Chelsea naps on my lap while her sister Maya runs after some birds. Rich, cherry-colored Wave petunias, looking full and vibrant as they cascade over the edges of the window box, decorate my patio. In the garden my pink gladiolas stand proud and pretty; they remind me of Mom and the flowers she grew against our back fence in Moose Jaw. I take in the rest of our garden with my eyes and feel a sense of accomplishment and contentment.

I lean back in the swing and look up at the sky; it's clear blue except for the white trail of a jet. I like the white against the blue sky; the inside of my house is painted with that classic, crisp, calming palette. Where is it going? I wonder as I watch the white trail move ever so slowly across the sky. I picture the passengers in uncomfortable, too-small seats thinking about their destination. I'm glad I'm not on the plane, no matter where it's going. I'm content to be in my backyard enjoying the warm late afternoon, not looking forward, not looking back, just savoring the simple blessings of the moment.

We are enjoying a record-breaking heat wave in the Pacific Northwest. Many are complaining about the heat, but Gerry and I enjoy it; it reminds us of summers in Kamloops and takes me back to childhood summers in

Saskatchewan. We are thankful we have air-conditioning in the house, but truth be told, we're only inside to sleep; whenever the sun is shining, we're outside.

Our life has been quiet since we moved to Washington. It takes time to build a community of friends, and I'm not good at that even in the best of times. My resolution to tell the truth is put to the test every time someone asks about my family; questions that are simple for everyone else require me to make a decision about what I will share.

Gerry and I are on a modified vacation this week, our own version of the "staycation" made popular in the economic downturn of the past year. It started on Saturday and resumes every day around 5:30 p.m., when we both arrive home from work. In anticipation of the warm weather, I've stocked up on all kinds of salads, cold cuts (six slices of mac-and-cheese, please), cheeses, fruits, and vegetables.

We spend most of each evening outside in the backyard in holiday mode. We move our chairs and lawn swing to the shaded area of the yard and surround ourselves with books, snacks, cold drinks, and magazines. Once in a while we hop into the hot tub—which isn't hot this time of year—to get wet and then dry off in the sunshine. It's one of the most relaxing weeks I can remember in a long time, and I realize how little it takes to make me content. Good books, good conversation with my husband, my little dogs, homemade potato salad, a cool breeze, a blue sky, a glass of cold Chardonnay, and the sound of children playing in the distance.

———◆———

Later, after we come in, I sit upstairs at my desk updating my blog. My desk faces the window, and I can look out at the cloudless sky and green laurels that grow around the perimeter of the backyard. A white fan on my desk whirs and oscillates; despite the air-conditioning, my upstairs office is warm late in the day. Though the window is closed, I can still hear the sounds of children playing in the yard behind us; I remember how hard it is to get children to sleep when it's still light outside.

One evening I feel compelled to do a Google search; ever since the inexplicable rejection by Uncle Bill at the auction, I periodically Google his name. This time, at the top the list of returned links, is one to his obituary. I sigh, click the link, and see his familiar face appear next to the text; he died in a car accident just two days earlier. I'm shocked by the news but not surprised that no one reached out to tell me.

I assume that no one has contacted Lori either, so I send her an e-mail with a link to the obituary. Over the years I've grown cautious about contacting her. She's like a porcupine; I know that at some level she wants to be close to me, and yet every time we are in touch or I try to create some semblance of a relationship, she pierces me with sharp words and accusations of perceived wrongs. Every time, I tell myself that this will be the last time I allow myself to be the brunt of her antagonism, but today, as the oldest sister, I feel responsible to let her know about Uncle Bill's death.

She responds the next day: "Linda, why is it that the only time I hear from you is when you have bad news? You could have waited until after my birthday. I guess I'm not going to have a happy birthday after all."

I assume she's referring to the fact that I was the one who let her know about the deaths of Mom, Aunt Edie, and Uncle Albert. As I read and reread her e-mail, I feel like a cartoon character doing a double take; I'm astounded. True, I hadn't thought about her birthday coming up, but we haven't traded birthday greetings in years. And it was never my choice to be the death messenger. I highlight her e-mail and hit delete.

I'm struck by the fact that with Uncle Bill's death, there is no one left who has known me all my life. Aside from Lori, whose presence in my adult life has been sporadic, Laurinda and Michael have known me the longest. I guess that makes me a matriarch.

Adoption File

Autumn 2009

For months I've been gathering and compiling all the information I have about both sides of my birth family. Makiya's birth and my own fiftieth birthday have encouraged a compulsion to document the family story that no one can tell but me. I'm blessed, as an adoptee, to have so much information about my genealogy; I know I have more history about my ancestors than many non-adoptees have.

Yet despite the satisfaction of documenting a rich and full family tree and the blessing of having family around me, a part of me remains empty and closed off, hurt, and afraid of rejection. Once, I thought I would fill the void if I could find my birth mother. Then I researched my family tree and where I came from, hoping it would help me feel secure about who I am. Later, I thought if I completed the picture by learning about my birth father and his family, everything would make sense and I would gain a sense of peace and rightness about myself. And along the way, I told myself that if I committed to truth, the shame would go away. Each of these things helped me find more of an identity, but none of them completely healed the little girl inside who had learned to adapt to what was expected of her and to pretend to be someone she wasn't.

I have all the answers now except one, the remaining gap in my story. When I think about the love lavished on baby Makiya and remember how she responded to her mom's attention at five months old, I grieve for baby Linda and wonder what her experience was at that same age. Did she feel a connection to someone as Makiya so obviously does to her mom? If she did, how did she feel when that person was no longer around? If she didn't, how could she ever feel secure and loved?

I need to find out about those first five months before I was adopted.

I find the contact information for Bev Jaigobin, who helped me find my paternal family years earlier. I take a chance and send her an e-mail asking if she can just fill me in on those first five months. Her response a few weeks later surprises me. The rules have changed in recent years, and she can provide me with a copy of my complete adoption file. I can hardly believe that I am going to see that fifty-year-old record.

On a sunny September afternoon a few weeks later, Gerry brings in the mail with the manila envelope I've been waiting for. He hands it to me, kisses me on the forehead, and says, "I'll be outside mowing the lawn." I know he's giving me time and space to open the deeply personal piece of mail.

I put the envelope down on the dining room table, suddenly reluctant to open it. What if this information isn't enough to satisfy my hunger for the truth and make me whole? This is the last piece of the puzzle, my last opportunity to find peace. I leave the letter and decide to fold the laundry. That familiar lump in my stomach reminds me that all is not as it should be, that there is truth that I am ignoring. Nevertheless, I continue upstairs with the laundry, ignoring what my body is trying to tell me.

When I finish folding the laundry and putting it all away, I look for something else that needs doing in the house to delay the inevitable opening of the letter. Finally, somewhat reluctantly, I sit down in the sunny dining room, take a deep breath, tear open the envelope, and pull out a bundle of paperwork attached by a large clip.

The first page is a cover letter from Bev Jaigobin. I scan it, put it aside, and turn to the rest of the papers. The first sheets are obviously taken from my case file; there are photocopied holes on the left edge of the page. This is the information I've waited my whole life to read.

February 18, 1959 (I was less than one month old)
Linda is a big girl for her age. She has lovely fair skin and nice dark-brown hair. Her head is well shaped, and her face is squarish. She has round,

plump cheeks which dimple up when she yawns. Her tummy is large and protruding. She has bright blue eyes. This is a bright, lively child.

March 13, 1959

Linda is a bright-looking child and very active. She is responsive, loves attention, and enjoys people. She seldom cries. She seems vigorous and active, smiles when spoken to, and tries to coo.

As I read, I feel a tenderness toward this little baby that I have never experienced before. The file in my hands proves that I existed from the moment of my birth, before I was adopted. The words are evidence that I was cared for, that I was born and not just dropped onto the Earth, as I once felt.

April 1, 1959

Linda was examined today for her adoption check. She has made a very good increase in weight. This baby's navel is protruding and apparently she has a rupture. The doctor showed the foster mother how to press in the bulge and pull the sides of the flesh around her navel over the center and then tape this. Her tummy is too large and so the doctor wishes to see her again in one month.

I think of Makiya's belly button and smile as I realize that this was passed to her from me. On the second page, I learn that I was admitted to the hospital when I was three months old and remained there for a month while tests on my kidneys, bladder, and stomach were done, and all came back with normal results.

Halfway down the second page I read more words that calm me.

June 5, 1959

Linda was placed on probationary adoption with Edward and Laura Brauer of Moose Jaw. The baby looked very lovely in a little blue dress and was the picture of a healthy contented baby. Her new parents were very pleased with her. The placement was comfortable and relaxed. The foster mother is to be commended on the job she has done with this baby.

I gave that same little blue dress to Laurinda months ago, not realizing it was the one I wore when I joined my family. The last sentence of this entry touches me deeply; I had a foster mother who cared for me in a way that warranted commendation from the social worker.

I was cared for—from the beginning.

There's more. Further in the file I find the intake slip filed when I was made a ward of the court one week after my birth. There is a notation about Mary: "Mother is quite disturbed in separation from child."

I put the file down on top of the table, lean back in my chair, and close my eyes. She was upset about giving me away.

I have very deliberately distanced myself from thinking about the day I was born; I have never wanted to consider how Mary must have felt. My deliberate disinterest and then later my anger at her have protected me. If I don't get too close, she can't hurt me.

Yet reading these words—"Mother is quite disturbed in separation from child"—softens my heart and allows me to feel compassion for my birth mother. Of course it must have been hard for her. How could it not have been? The words in black and white on the page in front of me allow me to believe it to be true. Reading about Mary's heartache makes me feel less rejected. I pick up the file again and continue reading.

June 17, 1959

Linda is the first child in this family, and Mr. and Mrs. Brauer have both been thrilled beyond words with this baby. Mrs. Brauer has taken over very capably and calmly as mother.

I consider how my twenty-nine-year-old mom must have felt to receive the precious gift of a daughter. And for the first time, I consciously accept that the precious gift was me.

I set the papers aside, and peace falls over me like a warm blanket. Part of the reason for my grief was that I felt abandoned and unloved by my birth mother. Now, as I feel compassion for her and allow myself to open up, I discover that I am beginning to heal. I experience what it's like to feel completely wanted and loved from the beginning of my life.

I remember Mary's gold locket that I tucked away in the back of my drawer and the matching locket that belonged to Mom, and I recall my words to Gerry. There is, I realize, a way to honor all the women who cared for me—Mary, the unnamed foster mother, and Mom.

Tomorrow I will go shopping for a chain so I can wear the two lockets together.

Mary and Frank

Reading my adoption file allows me to piece together the story of my birth parents.

Mary was married in 1949, when she was twenty-nine years old, in Chilliwack, British Columbia, to John Gunther. In pictures taken on that day, she does not have the dreamy look of a young bride in love. Perhaps as she stood next to her tall and slender new husband, she had a sense of what lay ahead, because after just a few months of marriage, amid claims Mary made of domestic violence, the couple separated. They had no further contact with each other but were never legally divorced.

Mary supported herself by working as a domestic for a series of widowers and bachelors. Perhaps she inherited the wanderlust of her Mennonite grandfather, who took his family from Russia, to Canada, to the United States, and back to Canada again, because she never stayed in one place for very long. Sometimes her relationship with the men she worked for went beyond the bounds of employer and employee, and by the time she met Frank Mosher, she had given birth to a son, Donald, who had been adopted by her sister Esther, and she was raising a three-year-old son, Merlin, supporting the two of them with welfare and a Mothers Allowance from the government.

Frank was a bitter and angry man. He had married at twenty-two, and over the course of nineteen stormy years, he and his wife had had four children. When Frank's wife left him for the last time, he continued to live and work on the family farm in southern Saskatchewan.

Mary answered an advertisement he placed for a live-in housekeeper after his wife left, and it wasn't long before they sought comfort in each other's arms. In the spring of 1958, three months after she started working for Frank, Mary learned she was pregnant. If she entertained any romantic illusions of building a family with him, they were swiftly put to rest when he refused to acknowledge the child as his own and Mary was forced to leave his home.

She contacted the department of social welfare that summer to arrange for her unborn child to be adopted. The social worker noted that Mary spoke very little about her unborn child; she seemed more concerned about her young son and appeared to feel sorrier for herself. Perhaps the appearance she gave of being disinterested in her baby was her way of protecting herself because she did not expect to keep the child.

On January 27, 1959, after eight hours of labor and with the assistance of forceps, Mary delivered a full-term baby girl weighing eight pounds, fourteen and a half ounces. She named her Linda Louise Gunther.

———

On March 24, 1959, the temperature in Regina Saskatchewan was barely above freezing and the forecast was for snow; winter was not yet over. It had been a difficult winter for Mary, being alone and pregnant and then giving birth to her daughter and surrendering her. She struggled with a depression so severe that she was prescribed medication for it.

The custom in those days was for a woman to go before a judge in order to sever her rights to a baby; it was also the custom for the infant to be present at the time. I imagine the judge looking at her sympathetically, trying to set her at ease, knowing the facts but still asking the questions for the record. I imagine him looking at the baby in the foster mother's arms, unable to prevent himself from smiling at the sight of her big blue eyes.

"Do you recognize the baby in court?"

Mary, perhaps with tears in her eyes and a lump in her throat, responds affirmatively.

"Are you the mother of this child?"

"Yes," she may have responded quietly, feeling the shame of her circumstances.

"What do you intend to have done with her? Can you keep her yourself?"

"I would like to, but I can't."

"Can you tell the court why you feel you cannot look after this baby?"

"Because I'd rather she had two parents instead of one."

"Do you understand that if you are unwilling to care for this child, and if we proceed with adoption, you will never be able to have her returned to you? Have you had enough time to think about this decision?"

"It's not that I'm unwilling to look after her. It's not what I want; it's what's best for her."

Mary signed the consent form to place me for adoption that day, but since she was still legally married to John Gunther, the department needed to seek his consent also. Two months later, the court received it, and I was made available for adoption.

And it was then that my mom, Laura, received the phone call that would change all our lives.

Closure

January 2010

I'm sitting in the airport waiting out a four-hour layover on my way home from Calgary. A few moments ago, I exchanged e-mails with Laurinda, took a cell phone call from Nicole, and chatted over my laptop on Skype with Gerry. If Mom and Dad could see how much the world has changed in the twenty-five years since they've been gone, they would scarcely believe it.

It's been one year since that winter morning when Makiya was born, and in a few weeks I'll close the book on fifty. I could never have imagined when this year started that I would find closure to my feelings about my birth family and my original tribe, and I couldn't have predicted the fierce love I would feel for a little redheaded girl who is just starting to take her first steps. It has been a year of miracles. It is as if the love I have for my children is concentrated and intensified into a kind of grandma-love I never knew existed. I wonder if this is how Mom felt when she visited us when Laurinda and Michael were babies. I wish she had lived long enough to see them grow up; I miss her still.

Makiya had her first birthday a few days ago, and I couldn't resist taking advantage of another reason to fly out for a visit. This trip, like the others over the past year, was filled with a double measure of joy. Six months before Makiya was born, Brandon and Nicole welcomed a precious son they named Jaxon, and I was able to spend time with both babies in Calgary. How blessed I am to have two beautiful and brilliant grandchildren.

A few weeks ago, as Gerry and I sat in a darkened church on Christmas Eve, I was overcome with the sweetest sense of gratitude and completeness. Reading my adoption file and penetrating to the root of the bitterness I had harbored toward my birth mother, replacing it with compassion for her, made it possible for me to have compassion for myself and to forgive myself. Once I forgave myself, I was able to allow myself to open up enough for the love of God to touch me deeply.

I am not the same woman I was a year ago. I no longer feel driven to seek significance by *doing*; I'm willing to let some things go and to rest in just *being*. I'm taking better care of myself. I'm listening to that still, small voice telling me it's not too late to pursue my dreams. And I'm thinking a lot about legacy and what I want mine to be.

Makiya won't have to wonder who her ancestors were. Thanks to the efforts of certain members of my birth family, she will have a rich and complete family tree; she will know which tribe she comes from. I have work ahead of me to compile all of this information into a format that can be kept and passed on.

And I want to write a book.

The adoption climate is changing, and there is a lot of attention being focused on whether or not adoptees should have access to their birth certificates and family history. I want to be part of the solution. I want people to understand that it damages children when we ask them to deny who they were born to be and become someone else. I want people to know that when children are adopted into a loving and nurturing family, they are as much a part of that family as if they were born into it. And I want to be part of a movement that contributes to endowing the adoption experience with a spirit of truth and transparency instead of shame and secrets.

To those, like me, who grew up feeling shame about their origins and a sense of disconnection from everyone around them, who hold people at arm's length, afraid to risk rejection by letting anyone get too close, I want to convey the message that it's not too late to find truth, healing, and peace. With every year that passes, it's more likely that an adoptee's birth parents will die, making a face-to-face reunion impossible. But in most cases, it's never too late to learn the truth about where they came from and the circumstances of their birth and adoption.

I'm fortunate that the province of Saskatchewan provides non-identifying information on request and offers search services; however as of this writing, there is a two-year waiting list for those services. It's also possible for those adopted in Saskatchewan to receive a copy of their Registration of Live Birth, their original birth certificate. I am in the process of obtaining my own. To do so I have to provide consent from both birth parents, which in my case is impossible, so I need to seek that consent from others related to them.

I want to be part of the solution that leads us toward a healthy adoption climate. I believe change will come with education and compassion and that my responsibility, as one who was affected and who has found healing, is to do my part to help foster that change in a healthy and respectful way.

I hope my story can provide hope to adoptees that it's possible to find peace and healing. For those who make the laws, I hope my story illustrates the importance of providing adoptees with as much information about their circumstances as possible.

In my fifty-first year, I find myself with a new mission: to do my part to be an educator and a healer about adoption.

Epilogue

*R*elationships are complicated even in the best of times, and for an adoptee there is an added level of complexity. Though we may fantasize about a reunion that will restore our place in our family of origin, the reality is often different. These days, when asked how many siblings I have, I still pause before answering and consider if I should give the long or short answer. I think about how much explanation will be required if I give the long answer. But my resolve to live in the truth has not wavered, and invariably I give the long answer. I have four brothers and four sisters.

Today, I have limited contact with my maternal birth family. Merlin is deceased, and I haven't heard from or about Donald since our initial meeting. Wendy and I recently reconnected after a couple of years with no contact; as usual, we are able to pick up where we left off. I'm happy to report that as of this writing she is cancer free. My cousin Esther Zaccharias, who compiled the books about our shared family heritage, exchanges sporadic e-mails with me.

My brother Frank, my first contact with my paternal family, passed away after a brave and inspiring fight with cancer. I never had the opportunity to meet him in person, but from what I've learned of him through our sister Ruth, I know he was a man of integrity whom I am proud to call brother. Muriel, the widow of my brother Ed, who had died before I found the family, is also an adoptee who has been reunited with her birth family. She and I shared some fascinating telephone conversations in the early years of my contact with the family. Ed and Muriel's daughter Cindy, my niece, put a lot of work into compiling a family history for which I am very thankful. She and I have occasional contact on the Internet. Ruth and I connect regularly via e-mail and Facebook. I've had no contact with my look-alike sister Miriam since our initial meeting.

Lori and I are estranged.

On the day you were born your cord was not cut, nor were you washed with water to make you clean, nor were you rubbed with salt or wrapped in cloths. No one looked on you with pity or had compassion enough to do any of these things for you. Rather, you were thrown out into the open field, for on the day you were born you were despised.
Then I passed by and saw you kicking about in your blood, and as you lay there in your blood I said to you, "Live!" I made you grow like a plant of the field. You grew up and developed and became the most beautiful of jewels.
(Ezekiel. 16:4-6)

The Adoptees' Bill of Rights

1. We have the right to dignity and respect.

2. We have the right to know we are adopted.

3. We have the right to possess our original birth certificate.

4. We have the right to possess all of our adoption records.

5. We have the right to full knowledge of our origins, ethnic and religious background, our original name, and any pertinent medical and social details.

6. We have the right to updated medical and social history of our birth parents.

7. We have the right to personal contacts with each of our birth families, as all other humans.

8. We have the right to live without guilt toward any set of parents.

9. We have the right to treat and love both sets of parents as one family.

10. We have the right and obligation to show our feelings.

11. We have the right to become whole and complete people.

12. We have a right and obligation not to violate the dignity of all people involved in the adoption triad and to carry our message to all adopted children who still suffer.

—Author Unknown

About The Author

$\mathcal{L}$inda Hoye is a writer, editor, adoptee, and somewhat-fanatical grandma. Her work has appeared in an assortment of publications in Canada and the US. In 2009 her piece, *The Face in the Mirror*, won second prize in the Susan Wittig Albert LifeWriting Competition. She is active in the adoption community and is an advocate for transparency in adoption. She currently lives in the state of Washington with her husband and their two Yorkshire Terriers but Saskatchewan, Canada will always be her heart's home.

She maintains a personal blog at www.lindahoye.com.

12503586R00123

Made in the USA
Charleston, SC
09 May 2012